The Bilingual Advantage

The Bilingual Advantage

Promoting Academic Development,
Biliteracy, and Native Language
in the Classroom

Diane Rodríguez
Angela Carrasquillo
Kyung Soon Lee

Foreword by
Margarita Calderón

Afterword by
Chun Zhang

Teachers College
Columbia University
New York and London

Published by Teachers College Press, 1234 Amsterdam Avenue, New York, NY 10027

The Home Language Questionnaire is reprinted with permission of the New York State
    Department of Education, Office of Bilingual Education and Foreign Language Studies.

Release to include the poem "An Indian Father's Pleas" was granted by
    the author, Robert Lake, who has the publishing rights.

Examples of the Cognates in English, History, and Mathematics are reprinted from
    Herrera, 2010, p. 96. Used with permission of Teachers College Press.

The Biography Card is adapted from Herrera, 2010, p. 64. Used
    with permission of Teachers College Press.

The National Association for the Education of Young Children on Technology
    Guiding Principles (from NAEYC, 2012) is reprinted with permission of
    the National Association for the Education of Young Children.

The authors would also like to express gratitude to all those individuals who released original
    poems, reflections, drawings, and lesson plans included throughout the book.

Library of Congress Cataloging-in-Publication Data

Rodriguez, Diane, (Educator)
    The bilingual advantage : promoting academic development, biliteracy, and native language in
    the classroom / Diane Rodriguez, Angela Carrasquillo, Kyung Soon Lee ; Foreword by Margarita
    Calderon ; Afterword by Chun Zhang.
        pages cm
    Includes bibliographical references and index.
    ISBN 978-0-8077-5510-5 (pbk. : alk. paper)
    ISBN 978-0-8077-7267-6 (ebook)
    1. Bilingualism in children—United States. 2. Language acquisition. 3. Education, Bilingual—
    United States. 4. Language experience approach in education—United States. I. Carrasquillo,
    Angela. II. Lee, Kyung Soon. III. Title.
    P115.2.R64 2014
       404'.2–dc23   2013048568

ISBN 978-0-8077-5510-5 (paperback)
eISBN 978-0-8077-7267-6 (eBook)

Printed on acid-free paper
Manufactured in the United States of America

21 20 19 18 17 16 15 14   8 7 6 5 4 3 2 1

Contents

Foreword

It is most rewarding to see this book on bilingual instruction at a time when there is a resurgence of this topic! For a decade or so, the focus on English has prevailed, even in schools that had espoused bilingual instruction since the 1970s and 1980s. Emphasis on testing in English, as well as federal and state funding policies, attempted to erode the importance of learning in two or more languages. Nevertheless, this imposed R & R time only served to give the diehards more time to think, recuperate, and emerge with a stronger will to persist in sustaining a type of education that makes sense now more than ever.

The other exciting news about bilingual instruction is that for the past five years new pieces of research have strengthened it. There are scientific studies now that show how bilingual instructional designs and strategies can be effective, how they can align with content area standards, and how whole-school professional development designs can have amazing results for bilingual students/learners. This book highlights these important studies and their messages for policy and practice. The authors have the experiences, knowledge, mind, and heart to bring together a medley of information those policymakers, educators, and parents will find useful as new decisions are made on the cusp of Common Core State Standards, new assessments, and new approaches to learning.

For several decades, educators have touted the benefits of bilingualism. Today's workforce embraces bilingualism as well as biliteracy. This book brings together the latest research on the advantages of children learning in two languages and two cultures.

The role of the primary language (L1) has often been misunderstood and misinterpreted. Some elementary bilingual/dual-language programs give too much time to L1 at the sake of the second language (L2; in this case, English). Hence, bilingual students learning English rarely make adequate progress and become part of the long-term EL group in middle and high schools. This book is devoted to the type of learning and teaching within L1 that should prevent long-term ELs rather than produce them.

The authors address other types of practical knowledge. They detail the uses of L1 in different programs (bilingual and ESL special education) and how bilingualism can be developed in the content areas. Instructional strategies and student tasks are provided for the different programs.

The chapters for the different types of programs will be of particular interest to teachers and program developers. They present ways of identifying the "best" language for instruction within each program, going into specifics about identifying the students' language proficiency. They detail how to enhance the students' oral language foundation, the role of vocabulary in enhancing reading, the development of reading comprehension, and ways of helping students become independent writers.

Another unique aspect is the detail on how the native language can be used in the second language classroom as an instructional support. Teachers always want to know how to skillfully create a balance in these situations. The same conflict of balance occurs in dual-language programs and classrooms. A chapter addresses this, with guiding principles for dual-language instruction, implementation indicators, and a vignette of a dual-language school. The treatment of classroom assessment of biliteracy growth complements the instructional approach through a student growth portfolio and a classroom literacy profile.

Of particular interest today is the struggle to provide the best education possible for bilingual students in order to prepare them for the Common Core State Standards and the tests that are forthcoming. The chapter on integrating language and content discusses the role of developing background knowledge, building content vocabulary in the native language, and using thematic approaches to teach content areas. Examples for preparing students for a content lesson and for integrating content knowledge and literacy in mathematics, social studies, and science are given.

Whereas there is a long list of publications (books, articles, chapters in books, research summaries) on how to teach English to ELs/bilingual students, there are a limited number of resources that deal specifically with the native language instructional component. This is one book that focuses explicitly on primary/native language. This book will be a great resource for university classrooms that lack such resources for teaching courses in different native languages. Although most teacher education institutions recognize the importance of students' native language and acknowledge that native language proficiency is a strength in students' linguistic and academic development, the focus turns quickly toward developing English. With the onslaught of the Common Core, there is a danger of losing sight of this student strength. Therefore, teacher preparation programs need to "hang on" to key resources such as this and keep these beliefs at the forefront of effective education for language minority children.

Margarita Calderón

Acknowledgments

Many individuals have contributed to the development of this book. First, we are grateful to the many English language learners we have had the privilege to meet as we visited schools and worked in classrooms. Their linguistic and instructional needs and strengths opened our eyes and minds, and gave us the motivation to prepare and write this book. We also thank the teachers and student teachers, especially from Fordham University Graduate School of Education and Touro College School of Education, who work with culturally and linguistically diverse students on a regular basis and whose ideas, questions, and experiences have helped to shape the content of this book.

We also thank two individuals who not only motivated us on a regular basis to complete the manuscript but also provided technical and editorial services: Dr. Kenneth Luterbach read each chapter and provided editing and content feedback, and Daniel Han provided technological and moral support throughout the entire process.

We thank Teachers College Press, especially Jean Ward, and editorial consultants for their guidance and suggestions throughout the entire process of the book.

The Bilingual Advantage

Introduction

The United States is a country of great linguistic and cultural diversity. This ethnic, racial, and linguistic diversification is evidenced most vividly among young and school-aged children. The diversity of language, culture, and ways of learning that students bring to the learning experience continue to inspire educators to meet greater challenges in their teaching role. School administrators and teachers are left with the responsibility of providing a quality and effective learning experience to all students, including those for whom English is not their primary or native language. A quality learning experience includes the provision of a first-class school curriculum, the identification of the best language for instruction, and the implementation of effective methodologies and instructional strategies.

In light of educational reform, current views of effective teaching focus on the understanding of human learning and the need for students to acquire advanced thinking and problem-solving skills, all of which are essential to succeeding economically in a competitive international society and culture. Therefore, the linguistically and culturally diverse school population must be provided with opportunities to learn the same challenging content and high level skills that school reform movements advocate for all students.

Linguistically and culturally diverse students in the United States reflect a variety of language backgrounds and language proficiencies. These students are commonly referred to as "English learners" (ELs), "English language learners" (ELLs), "bilingual learners" (BL), "emergent bilinguals" (EB), English as a Second Language (ESL) students, or "limited English proficient" (LEP). These terms are not employed universally; some individuals show preference for one term over the others based on language conceptualization, role, and instructional emphasis. Some of these students were born in the United States and others were born outside the United States. Some of these students are enrolled in bilingual programs; some of them are enrolled in mainstream English classrooms and receive English language development through ESL instruction; others are enrolled in English-only instruction. These students fall on a broad continuum of language proficiency, ranging from entirely monolingual in the non-English language, to balanced bilingual in the home language and in English. There is also diversity in the primary language and literacy at different levels of development.

Many of these students have neither the experience nor the opportunity to be able to function in all-English classrooms. Therefore, using students' native language as a tool for instruction is important for academic achievement and self-esteem, as well as for learning a second language. Most of the current literature points to the idea that the native language, if mastered, plays an influential role in the academic development of students. In addition, there is a need to expand these students' education not only by strengthening their primary language and adding a second language, but also by offering instruction in other languages that are useful and sometimes necessary in today's international economy and society. There is also a renewed sense of recognition and pride in ethnic heritage and ancestral languages, which encourages a shift toward bilingual education. As for those students whose mother tongue is not English, there is an even stronger rationale for being taught in their primary language while learning English.

In writing this book, we took some time to consider the terminology we wanted to use to identify the group of bilingual students learning English whom we are writing about. We reflected on the book's purpose, focus, and audience, and reviewed influential literature written by educational researchers (Diane August, Ellen Bialystok, Margarita Calderón, Virginia Collier, James Crawford, Jim Cummins, David Freeman, Yvonne Freeman, Kenji Hakuta, Stephen Krashen, Carlos Ovando, David Ramirez, Sonia Nieto) on the topic of bilingual education. We eventually decided that the term that suited these students best is *bilingual students*. Our conceptualization evolves from the perspective of a range of bilingual and biliterate students (the emergent bilingual, the transitional bilingual, and the balanced bilingual). These terms are further explained in Chapter 1. Due to the fact that in United States, these students are learning English and in English, government agencies usually label them as "English language learners" (ELLs), a term that is used in the literature to refer to students who are learning English. However, the term "bilingual students" reflects a more appropriate identification indicating that most of these students are learning in two languages.

Bilingual education has two primary language components: native language instruction, and English as a Second Language (ESL) instruction. Although there is a long list of publications (books, articles, chapters in books, research summaries) on how to teach English to these students, there are a limited number of resources that deal specifically with the native language instructional component. The purpose of the book is to provide information on native language teaching and learning and, specifically, to emphasize the native language component of bilingual education programs as a critical element for learning. In bilingual classrooms in the United States, instruction is implemented through two languages: English and the native language of the students, as long as there are more than 20 students of the same language in one grade (on occasion, two contiguous grades are combined). Native language indicates the students' home language (e.g., Chinese, Spanish, Korean, and Haitian Creole). How much instructional time is allotted for English and the native language depends on the type of bilingual program.

The intended audience for this book is primarily K–8 policymakers, teacher educators, teacher candidates, administrators, teachers, and parents who are involved in the education of linguistically and culturally diverse students. All educators need to recognize the importance of students' native language, acknowledging that native language proficiency is a strength in students' linguistic and academic development, develops a strong literacy foundation, and strengthens the bonds between home and school. Efforts should be made to seriously consider the teaching and learning of native languages.

Included in this book are a variety of instructional activities as well as student tasks that represent the language and cultural diversity of bilingual students enrolled in bilingual programs in the United States. In order to provide valid examples and translations, we asked the help of native speakers' practitioners of these languages (i.e., Spanish, Chinese, Korean, Haitian Creole, Hindi) to provide feedback on the language appropriateness of the instructional applications provided throughout the book. These practitioners became an advisory group, providing feedback on the language appropriateness of the instructional applications provided throughout the book.

ORGANIZATION OF THE BOOK

The book begins with an introductory chapter on the benefits of bilingualism, describing the cognitive, academic, and social benefits of bilingualism and biliteracy. Chapter 2, Native Language Instruction in the Classroom, provides a rationale for teaching bilingual students in their primary language, and presents the cultural, linguistic, and academic benefits of native language instruction as well as instructional strategies in facilitating the implementation of native language instruction in schools. It also includes a brief historical overview of bilingual education in the United States, and a list of the most popular types of bilingual education programs in United States. Chapter 3, Teaching Language Arts Using Bilingual Students' Native Language, begins to look closely at native language instruction from the language arts subject perspective, with a focus on moving students toward the development of biliteracy. Chapter 4, The Role of the Native Language in the English as a Second Language Classroom, encourages educators of bilingual students to see the role of the native language as a resource in the second language English as a Second Language (ESL) classroom. This chapter describes effective methods and strategies for providing comprehensible instruction using the native language to make ESL lessons and curriculum more cross-cultural and useful in both the teaching and learning process. Chapter 5, Native Language Instruction in Dual-Language Programs, provides a general overview of dual-language program implementation with emphasis given to the area of native language curriculum, instruction, and assessment. It provides a vignette of a dual-language school, listing the strategies and activities to use to promote native language literacy. Chapter 6, Promoting Native Language Instruction in the Special Education Classroom, provides an overview of the instructional needs of bilingual learners with disabilities and describes effective learning environments, instructional considerations, and strategies in teaching language, literacy, and the content areas in students' strongest language. Chapter 7, Using Bilingual Students' Native Language in the Content Areas, discusses the importance of integrating language and content, stressing academic language, background knowledge, and cultural literacy, supported by concepts, processes, skills, and recommended instructional strategies. Chapter 8, Technology in the Native Language Classroom, presents a framework for using technology in the native language classroom. It recommends technology resources to enhance teaching and learning.

MOVING FORWARD

We realize that interest in the topic of native language instruction is growing, and that there are many issues that remain to be addressed. We encourage other educators to continue to investigate and write on native language instruction in the different programmatic settings, and to collect data on the long-term benefits of its implementation. The population of linguistically and culturally diverse learners will continue to challenge educators to meet their linguistic and academic demands. We hope that this book is the beginning of a greater effort to meet those challenges.

1

Benefits of Bilingualism

I grew up in the Bronx with my Puerto Rican parents
I had papi, mami and abuelita speaking Spanish to me,
and when I turned five, I was ready to go to school,
to read, write, draw pictures and become a salsa singer
like Abuelo, who is in heaven today, singing the salsa blues.

I woke up very early, the day I started school
Mami took me to school, finding one close to home.
We arrived early, Mami wanting to see Miss Marrero first,
Miss Marrero said: Yes, I will teach in Spanish and English too,
Mami's face relaxed, smiled and became very confident
Toñito is ready and capable to learn in these two languages.

Mami signed all the paperwork she was asked to complete,
kissed me, hands together, took me to Miss Marrero's class.
The teacher said: "Bienvenido!" And just Mami left,
other kids were crying, scared of being in school
but not me, since Miss Marrero was there for me.

What a wonderful year I had in Miss Marrero's kindergarten class,
I learned to count, read, write, draw; music class after three.
I learned about my family, my ancestors, also about myself,
never questioning which of the languages to use
although I kept using Spanish, trying not to forget it.

As years passed, I successfully graduated from high school
Went to college, graduated with a music major
I thank Miss Marrero in guiding me to become bilingual,
fulfilling my dream of becoming a successful salsa singer.

(Angela Carrasquillo, "Being Bilingual")

The term *bilingualism* is generally used to describe the ability of an individual to use two languages in a variety of situations and conditions; *multilingualism* may be used to describe fluency in more than two languages. There is a considerable body of literature describing the advantages of bilingualism and multiculturalism for individuals and society. This chapter discusses that knowledge base in order to make explicit the core benefits of bilingualism, which will provide a foundation for the chapters that follow. These cognitive and academic advantages of bilingualism provide a strong rationale for teaching young bilingual learners in the United States for whom English is not their primary language in both English and their home language. Even if children and adolescents are not fully proficient in their primary language, enabling students to use their strongest language in school in addition to English will support them in their developing bilingualism, and also bring with it all of its cognitive, linguistic, academic, and cross-cultural benefits of bilingualism that we describe in this chapter. These benefits apply to any type of bilingualism in any context.

We hope that after reading this chapter, readers will find answers to questions about bilingualism and bilingual education, such as (1) What do educators, school administrators, and parents need to consider when trying to define the concept of bilingualism?; (2) What does bilingualism bring to the individual and to countries or regions that promote the use of two or more languages for instruction?; (3) What does the research say about the effects of bilingualism in children?; and (4) In the United States, does bilingual education have a chance to become a more significant instructional model in public schools?

THE COMPLEXITY OF BILINGUALISM

Bilingualism is not a new term. Throughout history, human beings around the world have spoken more than one language (often the native language from where they live and an additional one). For example, during the age of the Roman Empire, each region used its native language in addition to Latin, the language of the ruling class. What's more, Greek was the *lingua franca* in the eastern Roman provinces and became a familiar language to many Romans. Today, bilinguals are present in every country of the world, in every social class, and in all age groups. In shopping areas, customers speak different languages, and on occasion, employees will address customers in the shoppers' mother tongue. In places of worship, the language varies according to who is praying. There are neighborhoods in which two languages are commonly used for any number of social transactions, including for medical, financial, and educational purposes. Now more than ever, available technological, transportation, and communication advances facilitate the use of multiple languages within communities, societies, and the world.

Attempts to define the concepts of "bilingualism" and "bilingual" are not new either. Back in 1933, Bloomfield defined the term bilingual as native-like control of two languages. Although today we have come to understand that this is an ambiguous definition—considering the parameters of bilingual ability, bilingual proficiency, and bilingual usage—we recognize it as an important conceptualization of the use of two languages by an individual. We also affirm the notion that bilingualism is a complex concept to define. Although most dictionaries such as Merriam-Webster define *bilingualism* as "the ability to speak two languages," "the frequent use (as by a community) of two languages," and "the political or institutional recognition of two languages," these definitions are not sufficient because they do not take into consideration that defining who is or who is not bilingual is a difficult task since individuals who are considered or who consider themselves to be bilingual possess different levels and dimensions of bilingualism. That is, some individuals may be fluent or proficient in two languages but with different mastery levels of domains (phonology, pragmatics, syntax, semantics, and morphology), and with different proficiency of modalities (listening, speaking, reading, and writing). For example, individuals with a mastery of the syntax of a particular language may express themselves accurately in terms of the sentence structure but might demonstrate a limited amount of academic vocabulary. On the other hand, there are individuals who have a strong oral command of both languages but are limited at reading comprehension and at academic writing, or those who are actively fluent at understanding and reading two languages but demonstrate less ability in listening to them and speaking them.

Moreover, language cannot be separated from the context in which it is used. Bilinguals may use their two languages in different ways with different people (a relative, a priest, a teacher); for different purposes (to ask for information, to read a book, or to write a letter); and in different contexts (understand information provided by a school counselor, defend a point of view with a parent). For these reasons, we can say that at an individual level, there is a distinction between a person's ability or proficiency in the two languages and his or her practical use of the two languages.

BILINGUALISM AND THE BRAIN

Human beings have an interesting ability to learn more than one language, and this bilingual activity is mediated by functional changes in the brain. There has been discussion, debate, and investigation on how the brain organizes language in bilingual individuals and whether two different languages are localized in the same or in different areas of the brain (Dehaene-Lambertz, Hertz-Pannier, Dubois, & Dehaene, 2008; Petitto, 2009; Vaid & Hull, 2001). The dialogue has attempted to answer questions such as:

- In the brain of bilingual individuals, where is each language stored?
- How does the bilingual brain switch when confronted with two languages?
- What are the functional differences or similarities of a bilingual brain?
- How do the functions of the bilingual brain compare with those of a monolingual brain?

The main theme of these questions is whether language is organized and processed differently in the brains of bilinguals compared to monolinguals.

Although there are several points of view on how the two languages of bilinguals are stored and used in the brain, there is an accepted point of view indicating that different languages are organized partly in specific and separated areas of the brain (Conboy & Mills, 2006; Kim, Relkin, Lee, & Hirsh, 1997; Vaid & Hull, 2001). This is supported primarily by the fields of neuroscience and neurolinguistics, and further shaped by technological advances in brain imaging, as well as small-scale research studies. Vaid and Hull (2001) found that the left hemisphere dominated language processing for monolinguals, while bilateral involvement was pronounced in early fluent bilinguals compared with late frequent bilinguals. Thus, bilinguals appear to be less left-laterized than monolinguals, suggesting that similar or identical regions of the brain serve both languages. However, when bilinguals are going back and forth between their two languages, in the bilingual mode, individuals show significantly more activity in the right hemisphere than monolingual speakers, particularly in a frontal area called the dorsolateral prefrontal cortex (the source of the bilingual advantages in attention and control).

In fact, the structure of the human brain is altered by the experience of acquiring a second language. Acquiring a second language increases the density of gray matter (brain tissue that contains information-processing cells) in the left inferior parietal cortex, and the degree of structural reorganization in this region is modulated by the proficiency attained and the age of acquisition (Mechelli, Crinion, Noppeney, O'Doherty, Ashburner, Frackowiak, & Price, 2004). Bilingual adults have denser gray matter, especially in the left brain hemisphere, where most language and communication is controlled. The assumption is that the density of gray matter increases with second language proficiency.

Factors such as age, manner of language acquisition/learning of the language, level of proficiency, and the linguistic environment or setting directly affect a bilingual individual's development and brain function. In both behavioral and brain imaging studies, it has been found that the age at which a child is exposed to a second language has a significant impact on his or her dual-language mastery. Bilingual exposure at an early age has a positive and long-term impact on multiple aspects of a child's development. Petitto (2009) mentioned that as adults, these bilingual individuals, in addition to their good behavioral performance on language tasks, also show that their brains process the two languages in a similar manner, and identical to monolingual adults. The effect is strongest in people who learned a second language before the age of 5 and in those who are highly proficient at their second language. This finding suggests that being bilingual from an early age significantly alters the brain's structure; in other words, bilingualism requires a fundamental reorganization of the entire language system in the brain.

There is also another line of research that suggests that being bilingual can combat the cognitive decline that comes with aging and may delay the onset of age-related dementia. Because bilingual people constantly switch from one language to another or suppress one language to speak in the other, their brains may be better prepared to compensate through enhanced brain networks or pathways when Alzheimer's sets in (Schweizer, Ware, Fischer, Fergus, Bialystok, 2011). Speaking two languages may increase blood and oxygen flow to the brain and keep nerve connections healthy. For this reason, the brains of bilingual people have a constant mental workout in this particular region of the brain (Bialystok, Craik, Klein, & Wiswanathan, 2004). People who speak more than one language fluently throughout their lives have better problem-solving skills, better attention, improved executive function, and reduced risk and severity of Alzheimer's disease and dementia (Bialystok, Craik, Klein, & Wiswanathan, 2004).

SOCIAL ADVANTAGES OF BILINGUALISM

Current economic, political, and social trends are moving toward an even more connected world, which are influencing the use of language and communication. The political dominance of English as a world language has meant more pressure toward knowing English. Bilingualism and multilingualism where one language is English are increasing globally. Bilingualism is often encouraged for economic, informational, employment, and social interaction purposes, as well as for increasing cross-cultural understanding. Due to common markets, international trade, military security, and ongoing travel, the ability to speak two or more languages is seen as facilitating the realization of all these activities. The importance of knowledge of languages in addition to English in media, communications, economics, and trade is well established and will be even more important in the future for individuals as well as for governments, companies, and other institutions and organizations.

A group of 25 bilingual professionals who were working in business-related fields in New York City were asked to identify the perceived benefits of their own bilingualism (Carrasquillo, 2010). The responses of this group provide a comprehensive list of the advantages of bilingualism to individuals, and in the long run, to society. Figure 1.1 presents the most frequent responses (60% or more of the respondents) of the group.

Bilingualism provides benefits to the individual and to the society; it promotes international unity and closeness, and it provides opportunities for members of a nation to demonstrate consideration and respect to members of minority language groups. The opposite will cause dissension, as the separatist movement in Canada attests. Allowing language groups to participate in the decisionmaking process affecting the whole society provides a sense of equality rather than denying them their existence.

Figure 1.1. Perceived Benefits of Bilingualism

Careers and Employment	Economy/Trade	Information Technology	Communication/Cross-Cultural Understanding
• Being valued on the job for the ability to communicate with a diverse range of customers.	• Opportunity to conduct business in the language of the customer.	• Direct and continuous access to global and international information.	• Transfer of knowledge, concepts, and vocabulary from one language to the other.
• Opportunity to move up within the same company or outside the company.	• Using the language of the customer is good business.	• Direct contact with people and organizations from different cultures and languages.	• Able to find solutions to problems by analyzing them through the two languages.
• Opportunity to work in a bilingual work environment, enabling people to work in a comfortable workplace.	• Businesses must have a larger bilingual workforce to meet to the needs of a global market.	• Ability to understand what information is being disseminated in other languages.	• Intercultural mediator in a variety of marketing situations.
• More opportunities for retaining a job.	• Having bilingual individuals is an advantage.	• Ability to use information in different ways.	• Ability to relate to co-workers from other regions by speaking their language and knowing something of their culture.
• Opportunities for travel.	• Provision of a smooth and friendly interaction with other businesspeople.	• Opportunity to translate/communicate information to colleagues.	• Ability to bridge the cultural gap through knowledge of the language and culture of other business groups.

N = 25

BENEFITS OF BILINGUALISM IN CHILDREN

Research conducted after the 1960s has provided information about the additive benefits of bilingualism. There is a strong body of literature (Bialystok, 1987a, 1988, 2001; Bialystok, Barac, Blaye & Poulin-Dubois, 2010; Bialystok & Craik, 2010; Bialystok, Craik, Klein, & Wiswanathan, 2004; Bialystok & Martin, 2004; Cummins & Mulcahy, 1978; Galambos & Hakuta, 1988; Goetz, 2003) documenting the advantages of bilingualism, specifically in the areas of metalinguistic awareness, cognitive development, academic achievement, and cross-cultural awareness and understanding. In the 1970s, research began to identify evidence of bilingual effects on metalinguistic awareness and cognitive development, specifically on how the learning of two languages in childhood changed the way in which children thought about language. Later on, during the 1980s and 1990s, another line of research examined the effect of bilingualism on school achievement, in particular on literacy and academic achievement. Since the 2000s, research has also looked at the effect of bilingualism on executive function.

Most of this current literature repeatedly states that speaking more than one language does indeed appear to have a beneficial effect on aspects of cognitive development, cognitive control, and academic achievement. In addition, there is a body of literature indicating that effective implementation of a bilingual environment at the school society level supports the development of language and enhances students' self-esteem and cross-cultural understanding (Alanis & Rodríguez, 2008; Calderón & Minaya-Rowe, 2003; Wang, Shao, & Li, 2010). The following sections provide a brief discussion of these four advantages of bilingualism: metalinguistic awareness, cognitive development, academic achievement, and cross-cultural awareness.

Bilingualism Promotes Metalinguistic Awareness

Metalinguistic awareness refers to the process of using language as an object of thought; the ability to reflect upon and manipulate structures of spoken language (Tunmer & Myhill, 1984). It is the explicit knowledge of linguistic structure and the ability to access it intentionally. Such abilities are crucial to children's development of complex uses of language and the acquisition of literacy (Bialystok and Craik, 2010). Metalinguistic awareness relies mainly on two skill components: analysis of linguistic knowledge and control of attention processes. Research suggests that bilinguals, in contrast to monolinguals, are more metalinguistically aware and divergent thinkers (Bialystok, 2001; Cromdal, 1999; Goetz, 2003; Tunmer & Myhill, 1984). A heightened awareness of meaning of language and structure leads to a more analytical orientation toward language.

The analytical orientation toward language develops through the organization of the two language systems (Galambos & Goldin-Meadow, 1990; Tunmer & Myhill, 1984). Bilingual children receive more linguistic input, requiring a greater amount of linguistic analysis to understand it. It has been noted that having words in different languages may give an individual a wider variety of associations, rather than having a label in just one language. The different connotations and ideas around a word in different languages allow a child to build a more complex understanding of the word at a younger age. For example, a bilingual (Spanish/English) child who has acquired the labels of "ambiente" (Spanish) as well as "environment" (English) may be more capable to associate the concept of "surroundings," and to apply it to a setting, a situation, or a location. This is also due to "bicultural existence" that gives children the opportunity to associate several concepts with these labels.

Cummins and Mulcahy (1978) compared students from three language groups, monolinguals plus bilinguals, on a set of metalinguistic tasks to assess their ability to analyze linguistic structures and detect ambiguities, and to understand the arbitrary nature of linguistic labels. They found that bilingual children performed better than the monolinguals on most tasks. Bialystok (1988) also compared monolingual and bilingual children, and she found that bilingual children had better control of linguistic processing than monolinguals, and that those bilingual children with higher proficiency in their second language had better analytical skills than the children of lower proficiency.

Bilingualism Promotes Cognition

The literature on the cognitive advantages of bilingualism in bilingual children has focused on two main points: (1) mind development; and (2) the promotion of the executive functioning.

Mind Development. There is a conclusion, founded on studies conducted mainly with children, that bilingualism improves mind development. For example, Goetz (2003) found that bilingual children performed better (had the ability to learn successfully) than monolinguals, and he attributed their success to better inhibitory control, stronger metalinguistic skills, and a greater sociological understanding than their monolingual counterparts. Similarly, Bialystok and Hakuta (1994) concluded that the benefits from being bilingual go much further than simply knowing two languages. According to them, the structures and thoughts of the two languages are so different, it forces the child to think in more complex ways than learning only in one language.

Bilingualism also promotes divergent and creative thinking. A creative and divergent individual is one who thinks imaginatively, is an open and free thinker, and who is able to see more than one possible solution to a given task.

Executive Functioning. One of the most significant cognitive developments in early childhood is the emergence of the executive function system (Diamond, 2002), which is the basis for higher thought, including control of attention, working memory, and multitasking (Bialystok, 1988; Bialystok & Craik, 2010; Bialystok & Martin, 2004; Cromdal, 1999; Galambos & Goldin-Meadow, 1990), involving processes for attention, selection, inhibition, shifting, and flexibility (Bialystok, Barac, Blaye, & Poulin-Dubois, 2010) that are at the center of all higher thought. It has been found that bilingual children are superior to monolingual children on measures of cognitive control of linguistic processes, and that they develop control over executive processes earlier than monolingual children (Bialystok, 1999; Bialystok & Craik, 2010). Advantages to bilingual executive function can be seen on verbal and nonverbal tasks and processes. For instance, Bialystok (1999) conducted a study with bilingual and monolingual children with similar receptive vocabulary and memory span, and these children were asked to perform the dimensional change card sort task and the moving word task. Bilingual children outperformed their monolingual peers on both tasks.

Bialystok, Barac, Blaye, & Poulin-Dubois (2010) investigated the effect of bilingualism on the cognitive skills of young children. They compared the performance of 162 children who belonged to one of two age groups (3 years old and 4.5 years old) and one of three language groups (monolingual English speakers, monolingual French speakers, and bilingual speakers of English and one other language). The study participants were compared on a series of tasks examining executive control and word mapping. The bilingual children obtained higher scores than both groups of monolinguals on tests of executive functioning. Another study conducted by Bialystok and Martin (2004) showed that bilingual children outperformed monolinguals when card sorting was based on a perceptual, as opposed to a semantic, feature of the stimulus, indicating greater attention control and ignoring irrelevant perceptual information.

Bilingualism Promotes School Achievement

Research on how bilingualism promotes school achievement has addressed two main areas: (1) literacy and biliteracy; and (2) content area development. Here, we address the area of literacy and biliteracy development.

Literacy and Biliteracy Development. Hornberger (2003) defines biliteracy as any and all instances in which communication occurs in two or more languages. Different forms and levels of biliteracy develop in different social contexts, resulting in varying levels of reading and writing proficiency in two or more languages. A study conducted by Bialystok, Luk, and Kwan (2005) showed the impact of knowing one language and writing system on learning another. They compared a group of monolinguals and three groups of bilinguals with different relationships between English and the second language: Spanish-English bilinguals (alphabetical, same script), Hebrew-English bilinguals (alphabetical, same script), and Chinese-English bilinguals (different scripts). The results showed that Spanish-English and Hebrew-English biliterates had the highest levels of literacy. Their interpretation of the results is that bilingualism has two effects on early acquisition of literacy: (1) a general understanding of reading and its basis in a print system; and (2) the potential for transfer of reading principles across languages. All bilinguals showed an advantage in these areas over monolinguals, but the more similar the two languages were, the greater the advantage. It appears that bilinguals understand the symbolic representation of words in print earlier than monolinguals, as they see words printed in two separate ways. This implies that these abilities may facilitate the early acquisition of reading.

When biliteracy is encouraged in children, and if using a similar writing system, some literacy skills and strategies from the first language transfer to the second language. While the vocabulary, grammar, and orthography may be different, skills in decoding and reading strategies transfer from first language literacy to second language literacy. For instance, concepts of print and comprehension strategies easily transfer from first to second language literacy (e.g., scanning, skimming, contextual guessing of words, skipping unknown words, reading for meaning, making inferences, monitoring, predicting, recognizing the structure of texts, and using background knowledge about the text). In languages with different writing systems, such as English and Korean, bilinguals still can transfer some skills and strategies (Bialystok, 1987b, 1997, 2001). A study conducted by Bialystok, Luk, and Kwan (2005) showed that bilingual children demonstrated some general advantage over monolinguals in their ability to decode written forms into meaningful units. Strategies that may be transferred include knowledge of text structure, visual-perceptual relationships, and readiness skills.

It is necessary to note that, in general, bilingual children have lower formal oral language proficiency than monolinguals, and they have smaller vocabularies, weaker access to lexical items, lower scores on verbal fluency tasks, and demonstrate more interference in lexical decisions (Bialystok & Craik, 2010; Bialystok, Luk, Peets, & Yang, 2010). However, these deficits do not affect bilinguals' ability to express themselves. Proponents of standardized testing need to understand this finding, especially when vocabulary and language tests of bilinguals are analyzed. Often, bilingual lower scores in these areas are frequently presented as a sign of low academic development. The lexical deficits (smaller vocabularies and less rapid access to lexical items) are more at the mechanical level, while the cognitive benefits are much more significant in learning and academic development, especially in the development, efficiency, and maintenance of executive functions and divergent thinking processes (Bialystok & Craik, 2010).

Content Area Development. The literature clearly states that using the native language as a medium for learning facilitates the acquisition of content, and at the same time, learning content develops language and literacy skills and processes (August, Artzi, & Mazrum, 2010; Carrasquillo & Rodríguez, 2002; Lukes, 2011; Mohan, 1986; Wong Fillmore, 2004). Academic language relies on cognition, conceptual development, and the more formal language used in textbooks and expository essays. Sherris (2008) notes that language and content require task-based instruction, and that the acquisition of knowledge, provided through academic language within the identified content area, includes concepts, vocabulary, grammar, and discourse. He recommends that teachers incorporate the following: (1) clear content and language outcomes for the identified lesson or unit; (2) constant use of the building of background knowledge; and (3) provision of learning tasks that promote the development of literacy skills (reading, writing, listening, and speaking) within the content areas. Using students' strongest language facilitates this integration since students have at least some literacy skill mastery. Bilingual students who speak their native language fluently and have developed age-appropriate literacy skills have increased opportunities to learn content knowledge, which includes facts, concepts, processes, and principles (Goldenberg, 2006, 2008; Viadero, 2009).

Bilingualism Promotes Cross-Cultural Awareness and Understanding

In addition to the academic and cognitive benefits, bilingualism also positively influences the affective domain. Encouragement in using two or more languages, especially if one is the home language, has an effect, not only on how individuals think, but also on how they feel, as it demonstrates appreciation and respect for cultural and linguistic diversity. Self-esteem is of great importance in motivating oneself to succeed in school.

Wang, Shao, & Li (2010) interviewed bilingual children in both of their languages, and they found that these children had different stories, memories, and personal reports based on which language was used in the prompt. This finding indicates that a person's cultural belief system and autobiographical accounts are influenced and accessed differently through different languages, and they actually correspond to a language.

Bilingual and multilingual individuals tend to be better able to understand and communicate with members of other cultural groups and are able to expand their own world by becoming knowledgeable of multiple cultures (Calderon & Minaya-Rowe, 2003; Carrasquillo & Rodríguez, 2002). Moreover, Baker (2006) stated that by providing students opportunities to learn through more than one language in school, it may help to reduce conflict and increase harmony among language groups. He theorized that in Canada, French-speaking children learning English, and English-speaking children learning French may help their parents and politicians to produce a more bilingual as well as a more integrated Canadian society.

APPLYING TRANSFERABILITY THEORY IN THE CLASSROOM

Transferability of skills from one language to another plays a critical role in the education of bilingual learners. It has been theorized that there exists universal linguistic characteristics and knowledge that can transfer from one language to another (Cummins, 1981; Ramírez, Yuen, & Ramey, 1991; Vygotsky, 1962). One of the benefits of using bilingual students' native language in instruction is based on the theory that students who have a strong proficiency in their native language have the ability to transfer cognitive and linguistic skills, processes, and strategies from that language to a second language they are learning. Cummins's underlying proficiency assumption is that primary and secondary languages have a shared foundation, and it is this foundation that provides the basis for transfer of cognitive language. Students can transfer to the second language content knowledge, literacy skills, and critical thinking skills learned in their primary language. Individuals only have to learn a new concept once; the concept does not need to be relearned in another language. What individuals have to learn is the new label (word) that identifies that concept in the new language (Cummins, 1981).

The same could be said for literacy. That is, the acquisition of a complex understanding of the functions of reading and writing in one language transfer readily to a new language. Once students have a strong language and literacy foundation in the primary language, learning a second language (learning English in the case of ELLs in the United States) builds on these students' native language. This foundation is important because it accelerates the acquisition of academic language in English. As Cummins (1984) noted: "Spanish instruction that develops first language reading skills for Spanish-speaking students is not just developing Spanish skills, it is also developing a deeper conceptual and linguistic proficiency that is strongly related to the development of English literacy and general academic skills" (p. 143). In other words, there is a cognitive proficiency, which is common across languages, making possible the transfer of cognitive and literacy skills from one language to another. Bilingual students who have a strong academic native language foundation may draw on the following skills and processes when learning in a second language:

- *Conceptual Knowledge*: Students bring a long list of learned concepts to the new language.
- *Subject Matter Knowledge*: Older students who have been exposed in their native language to specific content related to the social sciences (i.e., history, geography, politics), science, mathematics, and general knowledge bring that knowledge to the new learning experience.
- *Higher-Order Thinking Skills:* Students experience using the primary language to inquire, question, compare, analyze, and argue about a variety of topics.
- *Reading Processes and Strategies*: Students bring a variety of learning strategies to approach a broad range of reading texts.
- *Writing Composition Skills*: Students may have been exposed to writing about a variety of topics with different audiences and purposes.

When these skills are developed in the native language, students will transfer them to academic tasks conducted in a second language. For example, students' literacy in the native language can bring positive effects on literacy development in the second language.

Odlin (1989) views this language transference as the cross-linguistic effect or influence that two or more languages may have on one another and that the transfer may occur in either direction, between the native language and the second language or between the second and native language. A typical example is that children who learn to read in the primary language do not have to start from the beginning when learning to read in a second language. The first language helps children to transfer knowledge and capabilities to the target language, including concepts and linguistic processes, which promote better understanding of complex concepts of the new language and the content areas (Odlin, 1989). Genesee (1979) saw great advantages in teaching students to read in the language that they know best. Bilingual students who are proficient in their native language bring literacy skills that benefit their transferability to the target language. For example, vocabulary, grammar, decoding and reading strategies, as well as general writing skills, may transfer easily from first language to second language literacy (Bialystok, 2001; Carrasquillo & Rodríguez, 2002). Strategies such as scanning, skimming, contextual guessing of words, reading for meaning, making inferences, and monitoring are all transferable skills.

Transfer is easier and faster when the relevant unit or structure of both languages is the same, or where the two languages have linguistic features that are compatible, such as a similar alphabet, or grammatical and syntactical structures (e.g., *madre* in Spanish and *mother* in English). Languages with a Roman alphabet have greater potential for transfer due to the identical linguistic elements of their language structures. However, there are languages that, due to their linguistic structure, are more difficult to transfer to a new language (Thonis, 1986).

For instance, Yum (2000) has discussed differences between East Asian languages and English, especially Korean and English. The Korean language has many different registers or rules of usage for different social settings. These rules are applied according to the level of intimacy, the status of the persons involved, and the particular context (California Department of Education, 1992; Yum, 2000). According to Yum (2000), "These differentiations are manifested not only in referential terms but also in verbs, pronouns, and nouns. They result from Confucian ethical rules that place the highest value on proper human relationships and on propriety" (p. 68). For instance, in the Korean language, there are different ways to say "to go": *gan-da* (plain), *ga-shin-da* (polite), and *ga-ship-shi-yo* (honorific), indicating that "different levels of a verb are often accompanied by different levels of a noun" (p. 69). However, honorific rules do not play an important role in English. Other potential difficulties arise with the lack of articles and prepositions, resulting in greater difficulties when writing in English. Sentence word order follows the sequence subject, object, verb, but in English sentences word order is generally subject, verb, object. Thus, Korean students may encounter difficulties transferring linguistic structures from Korean to English, although they can still transfer the conceptual, cognitive, and literacy foundation.

We encourage teachers to promote and encourage the transfer of processes, concepts, and cognitive skills from one language to another in their daily teaching. For example, having students write in a dialogue journal as a daily routine is an activity that promotes transfer. This is an activity in which students write or record their daily experiences in learning. Nieto (2005) recommends that one way to support the use of the native language is to invite teachers to provide a time and place during the school day for students to work with a peer who speaks the same language. Students can play different roles, such as tutor or mentor. This is a great way to promote native language literacy since they work together (e.g., read and listen to stories together), using their native language as a tool for the interaction.

So what are the necessary conditions for promoting cognitive, conceptual, and literacy transfer?

- Adequate exposure to primary language in school;
- Promotion of additive bilingualism or dual-language programs;
- Challenging instruction that emphasizes deep conceptual and linguistic proficiency, first in the home language and using that foundation in the second language instruction;
- Using parents as language resources and motivating them to provide language and literacy experiences for their children in the home;
- Availability of classrooms that provide opportunities for active exploration through questioning, diversity of learning experiences and activities, and meaningful conversation interaction; and
- Classrooms in which thematic units, community topics, and multicultural literature are main components of the first and second language curriculum.

Cognitive and linguistic transfer demand highly focused classrooms, collaborative and creative instructional tasks, as well as active learning activities. Transfer also requires equal value given to first and second language development and academic growth.

A WORD OF CAUTION ABOUT LANGUAGE PROFICIENCY

There is a common understanding that the relationship between bilingualism and cognitive/academic outcomes is mediated by the level of language proficiency, and that the advantages of bilingualism need to be viewed from the perspective of balanced bilingualism. Several studies have found that the further the children move toward balanced bilingualism, the greater the likelihood of obtaining cognitive advantages (i.e., Bialystok, 2001; Cummins & Mulcahy, 1978). Cummins (1979a, 1979b) explains the interdependence of languages and cognitive ability in bilingual children through the "threshold hypothesis." The idea is that a bilingual child must achieve certain levels of proficiency in both languages in order to avoid negative developmental outcomes and show cognitive abilities instead. Cummins makes it clear that if the first language learned has not reached a certain threshold of competence, the child may develop "limited bilingualism," a situation of lower linguistic competence in any of the various languages acquired in comparison to monolingual children. Therefore, it is the attainment of adequate levels of proficiency, especially in the primary language, that leads to positive cognitive and academic benefits for bilingual children. Metalinguistic awareness, for example, is developed to the fullest when the two languages of an individual are developed to their highest proficiency (Cummins, 1979a, 1979b; Galambos & Hakuta, 1988). Those individuals with emergent bilingualism do not share the benefits until sufficient proficiency in both languages has been achieved.

Another point of view is presented by Diaz (1985), who found a strong relationship between degrees of bilingualism and cognitive abilities in children, even those with low English proficiency. This finding suggests that the efforts of learning a second language, rather than increasing language proficiency, leads to cognitive benefits. We do not see these two different points of view as polarized because, in both cases, proficiency in the first language and the mental processes in acquiring both languages are of extreme importance. We emphasize the findings of Cummins and of Diaz, affirming that proficiency in the primary language plays a key role in deriving cognitive benefits of bilingualism. This is a critical point to consider in the instruction of bilingual children, especially the emergent one. The primary language students bring to the classroom and the instruction they receive in making that language stronger play an important role in how those students will develop cognitively and academically.

TYPES OF BILINGUAL INDIVIDUALS

There are three main types of bilingual individuals: *emergent, transitional,* and *balanced.* Keep in mind that these three types have many other subtypes within the labels, based on the prior discussion of levels of domains and modalities. There are individuals who are balanced in both languages; others may be strong in one language and emerging in the second one; and there are individuals who are emergent in both languages. For the purpose of this chapter, we simplify the discussion by providing a general description of the balanced, the transitional, and the emergent bilingual, with an emphasis on the benefits of balanced bilingualism. Figure 1.2. provides a brief description of these three types of bilinguals.

In the category of the emergent bilingual, there are two subgroups worth noting: (1) *borderline emergent bilinguals;* and (2) *emergent bilinguals with learning disabilities.* Borderline emergent bilinguals are language learners with academic, learning, or language gaps (but not a disability) that significantly hinder their ability to benefit from a

Figure 1.2. Types of Bilingual Students

Balanced Bilinguals	Transitional Bilinguals	Emergent Bilinguals
Competence in both languages is well developed;	Proficient in one of the two languages (usually the home language), and show developmental progress in the second language;	Proficient or fluent in the home language with evolving development in the second language (English in the United States);
Fluent in two languages across various contexts;	Show fluency or proficiency (e.g., understanding, speaking) in some of the second language abilities;	At the initial process of learning a second language (English) in school;
More or less equally proficient in both languages;	May be able to use the two languages for different purposes and events;	Do not have mastery of the second language to meet curriculum standards in English
Able to cope with the conceptual and linguistic tasks of the school curriculum in two languages.	Do not demonstrate sufficient mastery of the second language to cope and excel with English curriculum standards.	

general education school curriculum. *Emergent bilinguals with disabilities* have cognitive disabilities that limit their ability to learn. These two groups of emergent bilingual students require specialized instructional support, services, and a diversity of learning opportunities and instructional modifications.

More and more, the current literature is making a distinction among the balanced, the transitional, and the emergent bilingual. This distinction is noteworthy due to the relationship among the level of bilingualism, cognitive ability, and academic development. Although the concept of "balanced" may exist at a low level of competence in the two languages (two relatively undeveloped languages), in general, researchers and authorities in bilingualism refer to balanced bilingualism as having "appropriate competence in two languages." Baker (2006) gives an example of a *balanced bilingual* by describing "a child who can understand the delivery of the curriculum instruction in school in either language, and operate in classroom activity in either language" (p. 9). Therefore, when the literature makes reference to balanced bilinguals, the assumption is that these are individuals with well-developed competence or proficiency in two languages. However, an important point presented in the literature is that rarely are there bilinguals who are truly equal in their ability to use their two languages; often, one language is dominant.

An individual's language ability, bilingualism is influenced by external factors such as age, manner of innate acquisition and the linguistic environment, as well as the country's or region's philosophy and practices of bilingualism. For example, the age at which individuals are exposed to the two languages and the nature and length of exposure are key factors in the development toward balanced bilingualism.

CAN BILINGUALISM HAVE NEGATIVE EFFECTS?

The perception of bilingualism has not always been a positive one. Early research from the 19th century to the 1960s suggested that bilingualism had detrimental effects on thinking, and that learning two languages in childhood was destructive to a child's cognitive abilities, especially intelligence (Darcy, 1946, 1963). This adverse effect occurred when the two languages were learned independently and the knowledge of learning one language (e.g., vocabulary, concepts, linguistic structures) did not transfer in learning a second language. Researchers advanced the notion that as more was learned in one language, less could be learned in the other. This theory promoted the idea that there is a finite amount of language that can be acquired, and that the pieces learned in each language cannot exceed that limit. For this reason, parents and teachers were encouraged to teach children in one language instead of cultivating the ability to learn two.

As years passed and researchers began to look more critically at bilingualism and its effects, new methodologies were employed to measure the cognitive and linguistic outcomes of bilingualism. Criticism that countered the older theories focusing on negative effects of bilingualism pointed out the following: (1) the older studies emphasized the measurement of intelligence as the main variable of bilingualism; (2) intelligence was primarily measured using standardized tests; and (3) bilingual and monolingual children were grouped together without controlling socioeconomic factors or proficiency levels. Recent research has carefully controlled these variables, emphasizing cognitive development rather than intelligence, adding a variety of measurement devices and controlling for socioeconomic factors. According to Cummins (1984, 2000), it is possible to explain the negative results of bilingualism on the language replacement trend of linguistic minorities where the minority language was being replaced by the socially dominant one. The controversy surrounding the impact of multilingualism on children is ongoing, attributing the lower linguistic skills of some children not to the effects of several languages but to the impact of other variables such as quality of instruction, as well as social and economic factors.

Still, today there are many individuals implementing educational programs who consider bilingualism as detrimental to cognitive and academic progress. Their concerns are founded on documented evidence of the delay of bilingual individuals in acquiring some formal aspects of the two languages, such as vocabulary (Bialystok, Luk, Peets & Yang, 2010). In the United States, opponents of bilingualism and bilingual education argue that using students' primary language other than English in instruction delays students' mastery of English, thereby delaying their learning of other subject areas as well. There are also individuals, especially at the educational policy level, who strongly believe that bilingualism tends to foment political and national divisiveness rather than strengthen a feeling of national unity. Others believe that the more opportunities individuals have to use the second language in the learning process, the more acculturated and nationally supportive these individuals become.

COUNTRIES WITH BILINGUAL EDUCATION PROGRAMS

Aside from countries like Canada that are officially bilingual, there are several countries (beyond the United States) whose governments allow and encourage, for different reasons, bilingual education in schools. These countries have different motives in educating through bilingual education, as well as varying student populations that receive bilingual education. Figure 1.3 presents a sampling of some of these countries:

Figure 1.3. Countries with Bilingual Education Programs (Outside United States)

Type of Program	Country
Programs for Foreign Language Instruction (Majority of students learning a foreign language)	Hungary: English Hong Kong: English
Programs for Immigrant Children	Norway: Turkish, Urdu, Vietnamese Netherlands: Turkish, Arabic
Programs for Indigenous Minorities	China: Korean Sweden: Finnish Australia: Gapapuyngu Mexico: Tzeltal, Tzotzil
Two-Way Programs for Language Minority and Majority Students	Denmark: Turkish, Danish Belgium: Spanish, Belgian Sweden: Finnish, Swedish Germany: Turkish, Greek, German Finland: Swedish, Finnish Canada: French, English Ireland: Irish, English

The acceptance and support of some type of bilingualism, especially at the policy level, gives hope that in the face of globalization and information technology, more countries, especially the United States, will provide policies or mandates supporting bilingualism and the use of more than one language for instructional purposes. It is painful to say that current policies suggest that the United States demonstrates resistance to recognizing (possibly for fear of losing unity) the richness that bilingualism brings to the individual and to the economy as well as the benefits for international trade and communication. Yet we do recognize that the situation of minority languages in the United States is different from that of minority groups in other countries. For most of the linguistic and ethnic groups in the United States (with the exception of Puerto Ricans and Native American Indians), the move to the United States has been voluntary and these immigrant individuals are aware that their mother tongue is not spoken by the majority of the population. In other countries, such as India and China, linguistic minorities have not emigrated—their ancestors have owned the land, and they and their offspring are native citizens.

IMPLICATIONS FOR INSTRUCTION IN THE UNITED STATES

Current research clearly presents a positive relationship between balanced bilingualism and bilingual children's cognitive, linguistic, academic and cross-cultural development. The question is—how far does a bilingual individual have to move up on the two language ladders to obtain cognitive advantages from bilingualism? This is an important question if we consider that in the United States, the majority of the bilingual public school population is enrolled in transitional bilingual education programs, and that these students are at the emergent bilingual level. The goal of transitional bilingual programs is not bilingualism and biliteracy, but merely a scaffold to support children as they acquire English. Our recommendation to educational policymakers and school administrators is to provide more opportunities to students to ensure that they become balanced bilinguals. In doing so, these students can fully profit from the many cognitive and linguistic benefits of bilingualism. Programs such as dual-language and developmental/late-exit bilingual programs (not merely transitional programs) focus on long-term bilingualism and balanced bilingualism, and should be the focus of bilingual education policymaking.

Nunley (2010) encourages the use of two languages in the classroom and promotes bilingualism in the teaching and learning process. Regarding social and instructional support for English learners, Nunley provided the following advice to teachers:

> Help them understand this incredibly valuable gift they bring with them to school. Encourage them to continue to use, speak and read, whenever possible, in both of their languages. Ask them questions that they can respond to in either language. Have them share stories, recall information and learn in both languages: "Tell me in English what you remember learning about the water cycle, and then tell me again in Luganda." Encourage their bilingualism. Help them celebrate their gift. (p. 2)

2

Native Language Instruction in the Classroom

I live in a monolingual country, with people of diverse backgrounds
with children and youth, raised within linguistic diversity
those who speak a language which is not the official, national one.
I am one of them, a competent speaker of Language One,
my primary, my ancestral, my mode of thinking, and my being.

Through Language One,
I find it easier to speak of anything connected with emotions
affective content, descriptions, imagery, complex feelings,
with a display of a strong range of meaningful and clear words
I dream, I count, I sing, I pray, and I share love around me.

Language One,
helps me to express my identity, beliefs, rituals, behaviors,
a manifestation, a symbol, a marker of who really I am,
index of a personalized past, homelands and histories,
a clear vision of my past, my present and my future.

Language One,
A demonstrated expression of community relationships,
sharing attributes, collective and individual friendships,
shared existence, with a wealth of organized experiences.
A view and interpretation of the universe,
With a unique and particular understanding of the world.

Language One:
You need to increase prestige within the dominant community,
promoting bilingualism, biliteracy and cognitive growth.
You are useful in instructing bilingual students,
helping them not to be alienated in American schools,
by those, that only see instruction through Language Two.

(Angela Carrasquillo, "Language One")

Native language instruction is the practice of teaching school children in their native language in addition to providing instruction in the official language of the country of residence. There is a strong body of literature that supports the need to teach students in their strongest language, which in most cases, is their native language (Cardenas,

1986; Carrasquillo & Segan; 1998, Cummins, 1981, 1989; Echevarria & Graves 2011; Slavin & Calderón, 2001). Using students' primary language as the main tool for instruction has advantages for teaching and learning, and teachers, teacher educators, and curriculum developers need to understand the research justifications and practical benefits of using the students' strongest language. In the United States, this understanding is particularly poignant since public school teachers instruct a significant number of students who do not have language proficiency in English, yet are forced to use this new language to learn the school curriculum (e.g., language arts and other subject areas).

This chapter provides a theoretical overview of the role of native language instruction in promoting the linguistic, academic, and cognitive development of bilingual students in the United States. The following questions serve to guide the discussion of the chapter: (1) What role does native language instruction play in the instruction of bilingual students in the United States public schools?; (2) What type of ethnic and linguistic diversity is reflected in U.S. schools and classrooms?; (3) What are the linguistic, cultural, and academic challenges students bring to and are faced with in the teaching and learning process?; and (4) What instructional strategies are effective in facilitating the implementation of native language instruction in schools? This chapter encourages educators to develop an appropriate teaching climate, curricula, instruction, and materials for succeeding in meeting bilingual students' linguistic and academic needs.

LANGUAGE DIVERSITY IN THE UNITED STATES

Language diversity in the United States has been maintained primarily due to the continuing immigration of individuals from non–English speaking countries, as well as from children born in the United States into non–English speaking families. The estimated number of linguistically and culturally diverse students in American schools is close to 5.3 million, or 11% of all the K–12 school population (Migration Policy Institute, 2010b). Those students speak a primary language other than English. Although the name or label used to identify these linguistically diverse students who do not demonstrate proficiency in English has shifted throughout the years (*linguistically and culturally diverse, limited English proficient, English language learners, English learners, bilingual students, emergent bilinguals*), the most commonly used term is *English Language Learners* (ELLs), followed by *bilingual students*. Figure 2.1 shows the top 11 states in the United States with the largest school enrollment for students who are not proficient in English.

The national population of students with a language other than English has increased dramatically. The state of California has the largest number, with an ELL enrollment of 24%, followed by additional states where ELL enrollments are more than 5% of all school students. In addition, ELLs are represented in almost all U.S. school districts. This student population is ethnically and linguistically heterogeneous, representing a diversity of countries and many language groups. The U.S. educational system has over 100 distinctive language groups represented in schools, and a significant group of those students are learning English as a new language. Over 73% of them speak Spanish as their first language, 3.8% speak Chinese (all languages), 2.7% speak Vietnamese, and

Figure 2.1. States with the Largest Percentage Enrollment of English Language Learners, Pre-K–12 (2007–2008)

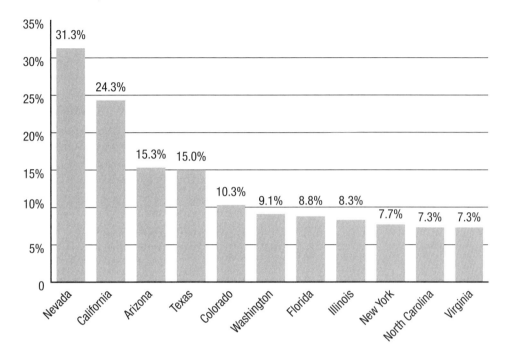

Source: Information from the Migration Policy Institute, 2010b.

2.1% speak French or Haitian Creole (Migration Policy Institute, 2010a). There is a long list of more than 100 language groups represented in the educational system, including, for instance, Arabic, Bangladesh, Burmese, Chinese, French, German, Hebrew, Hindi, Hmong, Italian, Korean, Ladino, Miao/Hmong, Native Hawaiian, Pidgin, Polish, Portuguese, Russian, Spanish, Thai, Urdu, and Welsh.

Linguistic diversity challenges educators to provide appropriate instructional programs and curricula in order to narrow the achievement gap between monolingual English speakers and linguistically and culturally diverse students. The following description provides an example of language diversity in the New York State school system.

The English Learner Population in New York State

The EL population in New York State has remained fairly stable over the past ten years, fluctuating between 6 to 8 percent of the public school population. In 2010–2011, there were a total of 238,792 ELLs in public schools throughout the state and an additional 84,746 ELLs in nonpublic schools. The majority of ELLs are concentrated in New York City (70%); the next largest ELL enrollment is Brentwood in Long Island (13%). The remaining four large city school districts (Buffalo, Rochester, Yonkers and Syracuse) together enroll 6% of the State's ELL public school population. ELL students speak nearly 200 different languages in New York State. The majority of ELLs speak Spanish followed by Chinese, Arabic, Bengali, and Haitian Creole. There are five other languages that make up the top 10, namely Urdu, Russian, French, Korean and Albanian. There have been some demographic shifts with Arabic and Bengali replacing Russian and Urdu. (New York State Education Department, 2011, p. 3)

Many stakeholders in U.S. school systems, including federal and state policymakers, teachers, and administrators, are concerned that linguistically and culturally diverse students, especially English language learners, are underachieving in the educational system, especially when compared to native English speakers. We wonder about the main causes for the achievement disparity between ELLs and native English speakers. We theorize that there is a combination of factors contributing to the achievement gap, including enrollment in low-achieving schools, placement in lower-ability classrooms, and lack of challenging curricula. We also theorize that, in many cases, the achievement gap is often due to the failure of schools to use students' primary language for instruction. In seeking possible solutions to the achievement gap, we call on educators in the United States to reflect on the language of instruction, the curricula, and the teaching practices provided to students with a variety of primary languages and a diversity of cultures.

BILINGUAL EDUCATION IN THE UNITED STATES: A HISTORY

The United States is a diverse country in which many languages are spoken by its residents, yet bilingualism is not promoted by government policies, mandates, or funding. In the United States, politicians, administrators, and policymakers have held various perspectives on bilingual education, indicating underlining shifts in ideology, preference, and practice (Crawford, 2004; Hakuta, 1986). Accordingly, the concept of teaching in two languages (English and a language other than English) is not a novel idea in the education history of the United States.

Early Acceptance of Bilingual Education

The United States has been a land in which many languages have been and still are spoken, beginning with the more than 300 native languages used before European immigrants arrived. The Italians, Germans, Dutch, French, Polish, Czech, Irish, Welsh, and Spanish immigrants brought with them their own languages, and up to the beginning of the 20th century, linguistic diversity was accepted and frequently encouraged through religion and private and public schools (Maltiz, 1975). For example, in the 17th century, Polish immigrants, in the first permanent English settlement of Virginia, established the first bilingual schools with subjects taught in English and Polish. In 1839, Ohio became the first state to adopt a bilingual education law, authorizing German-English instruction at parents' requests. Louisiana enacted an identical provision for French and English in 1847, and the New Mexico Territory did so for Spanish and English in 1850. By the end of the 19th century, about a dozen states had passed similar laws. Bilingual public schools existed and flourished in Cincinnati, Cleveland, and Milwaukee (English and German), Louisiana (English and French), and New Mexico (English and Spanish).

The Shift Toward Unity over Diversity

But in the first 2 decades of the 20th century, there began an animosity toward bilingualism and bilingual education that favored the elimination of languages other than English and started the decline of the promotion of bilingualism and bilingual education. People in power felt that the linguistic diversity reflected in society and in the school population could foment dissention and lack of national unity; many people believed that the English language was under threat. This hostility toward bilingualism continued into the 1960s.

The Second Movement Toward Bilingual Education

In 1963, there was a highly successful experiment in bilingual teaching in the Dade County School District in Florida, which was conceived to handle the influx of Cuban students in the Miami area at the time. By the end of the 1960s, many Cuban exiles had moved into Florida and enrolled their children in public schools. The Dade County School District was then faced with the problem of how best to teach large numbers of children who spoke only Spanish. With money made available from Cuban refugee funds, a bilingual program was set up at the Coral Way Elementary School in Miami. This bilingual program relaunched the promotion of bilingual education in the United States.

In 1964, the Civil Rights Act called for the establishment of equal opportunity for all people irrespective of race, color, or creed, creating the climate for the acceptance of languages other than English at the federal level. The findings of the mandate challenged school authorities to develop ways of providing equal opportunities for children of various ethnic minority groups who did not speak English. Members of Congress were also challenged to create legislation that would provide equal educational opportunities. In 1965, under pressure, Congress passed the Elementary and Secondary Education Act (ESEA) to help local districts solve some of the language problems found in their schools and to upgrade the educational opportunities for groups of students who were not succeeding academically, which put them at greater risk of dropping out. But it was the creation of the federal Bilingual Education Act (Title VII), an addition to ESEA, which was signed into law in January 1968 and provided funds to support the teaching of children and youth in a language they understood, that initiated a second movement toward the creation of bilingual education in the United States.

One of the main reasons for the federal decision to provide funding for the establishment of bilingual programs, specifically for children from lower socioeconomic status backgrounds, was that their drop-out rates were high due to academic failure. School districts submitted applications for federal monies to finance bilingual programs, including carefully worked out plans and objectives, to the U.S. Office of Education, Division of Bilingual Education. Funded programs had to be evaluated at the end of each school year in order to be eligible for continued funding. Projects were funded for a maximum of five years. Federal funds were available for teacher training, materials, and staff development.

In 1974, the U.S. Supreme Court ruling *Lau vs. Nichols* gave further momentum to bilingual education when the court held that San Francisco schools had violated minority language rights when they educated students in the same classes as other students without special provisions. The decision affirmed that Chinese students in San Francisco were not receiving special help with their language needs. The court further ruled that schools receiving federal funds must provide those students with the same opportunities given to English-speaking students, and that these students' opportunities would be equal to those of English-speaking students only if they understood what they were taught. The Bilingual Education Act and the *Lau v. Nichols* ruling mandated schools to at least provide some type of services to support limited English proficient students, though neither specified what type of educational program method or approach needed to be provided.

The *Lau vs. Nichols* (1974) decision in California as well as the Aspira Consent Decree in New York City (1974) are legal linguistic mandates that redirected educational communities that rejected the use of an inappropriate language of instruction in school. *Lau vs. Nichols* requires school districts to identify students whose native language is one other than English and to provide these students with instruction in a language they understand. In 1974, Aspira advocates used the *Lau vs. Nichols* ruling to push the New York City Department of Education to provide instruction in Spanish to those Hispanic students whose native language was Spanish. A significant number of bilingual education programs were established, with many of those programs using the students' native language and English for instruction. Most of these programs were transitional in nature (provided only until students were able to be proficient in English), although some additive or maintenance bilingual education programs (maintained regardless of students' English proficiency) were also established. With the fiscal support of the federal government, some states began to mandate some type of transitional bilingual programs or services (Massachusetts, 1971; California, 1973; Connecticut, 1973; Louisiana, 1968; New Jersey, 1973; New York, 1973; Pennsylvania, 1972; Texas, 1972). The largest language groups served were Spanish-speaking.

In 1978, the United States Congress reauthorized transitional bilingual education, allowing the native language to be used only to the extent necessary for a child to achieve competence in the English language. Federal funds could no longer be used for maintenance bilingual education programs. These federal policies went through the 1984 and 1988 ESEA amendments. In 1994, Congress passed the Goals 2000, Educate America Act and the Improving America's Schools Act, which continued the limited federal support for bilingual education programs.

In 2001, No Child Left Behind (NCLB) offered no support for native language learning and instruction, put strong emphasis on learning, accountability, and testing in English only, and created mandates for all students to be tested yearly in English. In 2009, the federal government established Race to the Top, a policy that continued the NCLB goals of transitional bilingual education programs.

The Debate Continues

Since the late 1960s, the merits and benefits of bilingual education have been repeatedly questioned. Although there is a strong body of research on the benefits of bilingual education, critics of bilingual education have claimed that there is little empirical evidence to support it and that bilingual education programs fail to teach students

English. This debate will continue in the United States until the society at large, which includes policymakers, recognizes that the ability to speak multiple languages is not a threat to national unity or national security.

On the other side of the discussion, there is a group of advocates and researchers (e.g. Ellen Bialystok, James Crawford, Jim Cummins, Stephen Krashen, Kenji Hakuta, and Virginia Collier) who have conducted research and presented arguments on the academic merits of bilingual education. These individuals argue that, for many students, the process of becoming literate and learning a new language simultaneously is overwhelming, and that bilingual programs help these students develop native language literacy first, which makes the transition to English smoother. Proponents of bilingual education argue that the bilingual approach will not only help keep non-English-speaking children from falling behind their peers in math, science, and social studies while they master English, but also that these students will learn English better than in English-only programs. Proponents stress that effective bilingual programs strive to achieve proficiency in both English and in the students' home language, calling for the establishment of more late-exit and dual-language programs.

A comment frequently heard about bilingual education programs is that parents who want their children to be educated in their native language will take care of it themselves by organizing after-school classes to teach their children. But this view ignores the fact that the majority of parents of children enrolled in bilingual education programs are not in a financial or educational position to arrange for this supplementary teaching. Because many parents cannot teach literacy in their native language, it is desirable for public schools to add this enrichment literacy goal to their school curriculum.

Another frequently made objection against bilingual education is related to cost. Although it is true that at the initial stage, money is invested in the acquisition of bilingual instructional materials, staff development, and the hiring of bilingual teachers, the benefits are worth the extra expense. When this issue of funding arises, we always pose this question: Since school districts must always pay for providing teachers and resources for all students, why should English learners not be served as well?

TYPES OF BILINGUAL EDUCATION PROGRAMS IN THE UNITED STATES

Currently in the United States there are three main types of bilingual education program models implemented in public schools: (1) transitional; (2) dual-language/two-way; and (3) late-exit/developmental. The transitional and dual-language models are the two most common in actual practice.

Transitional Bilingual Program

This program is intended to provide students with instruction in their native language only until learners can move into an all-English curriculum and to ensure that students do not fall behind in content areas like mathematics, science, and social studies while they are learning English. This program involves instruction in students' native language, typically for no more than 3 years. The goal is to help students transition into mainstream English-only classrooms as quickly as possible. The linguistic goal is English acquisition only. This is the most frequently recommended program from the federal government as well as from state and local educational agencies.

Dual-Language Program

This program (also known as two-way) is intended to teach literacy and subject area content in two languages. School instruction is provided in both languages, and the percentage of each language and the language to be used in each subject area is determined by the school or district philosophy. Dual-language programs generally begin in kindergarten or 1st grade and extend for at least 5 years, although some programs continue into middle school and high school. These programs aim for bilingualism (the ability to speak fluently in two languages), biliteracy (the ability to read and write in two languages), academic achievement equal to that of students in English-only programs, and cross-cultural competence.

Late-Exit/Developmental Bilingual Program

Instruction is provided in the students' native language for an extended duration (6+ years), accompanied by instruction in English. The goal is to develop literacy in the child's native language first, then to gradually transfer the skills into English and promote the use of both languages for instruction and learning. But this is an almost nonexistent program in U.S. public schools since neither the federal government nor states provide funds for its implementation.

BILINGUAL STUDENTS' LINGUISTIC, CULTURAL, AND ACADEMIC CHALLENGES

Students bring various academic backgrounds and skills; some students come with grade-level academic preparation in their native language while others are unprepared for the academic demands of school. These students face challenges that are caused by the varying levels of educational backgrounds, academic achievement, and language proficiency established prior to enrollment in U.S. schools.

Linguistic Challenges

There is research to support the notion that students who speak their native language fluently, and have developed age-appropriate proficiency and literacy skills in that language, have increased opportunities for mastering the school grade-level curriculum, including the acquisition and learning of a second language and mastery of the various school subject areas (Cummins, 1989, 1991, 2005; Echevarria & Graves, 2011; Ramirez, Yuen, & Ramey, 1991). Bilingual students need a strong language foundation, including basic vocabulary, knowledge of the academic world around them, and linguistic and cognitive ability to match with the instructional language and literacy demands and cognitive strategies of the grade-level curriculum (Carrasquillo, Kucer, & Abrams, 2004). Bilingual students have most of these skills in the native language that

Figure 2.2. Curriculum Demands and Academic Registers

Curriculum Demands	Academic Registers
Seek information	Complex features of speech
Summarize information	Reading a variety of texts
Provide information	Writing for different audiences and purposes

can ultimately be transferred to the grade-level curriculum and to the second language. This transfer does not occur until a relatively high level of proficiency in the native language and later on in the second language.

However, those students who have not developed high proficiency in their native language and who do not have the linguistic foundation to become successful learners may be challenged by the demands of the school curriculum. As students progress through the grades, the academic tasks they are required to complete and the linguistic contexts in which they may function become increasingly complex. Consider the linguistic functions as shown in Figure 2.2, which are demanded by curriculum and require particular academic registers.

Content instruction becomes increasingly more complex and abstract, and requires a different register for academic conversations. This perceived failure will prohibit students from developing interest and involvement in language and content area learning tasks, such as selecting problem-solving activities, using pair work, and language activities. Students need particular styles and modes of language to accomplish various academic tasks. And to do these academic tasks, students need a strong language foundation that includes, at least, grade-level vocabulary, advanced cognitive processing, and grade-level literacy to match with the instructional demands of the grade-level curriculum.

Cultural Challenges

There is an intimate link between language and culture, and the nature of language is closely related to the demands and functions that it has to serve. Understanding and respecting bilingual students' heritage and culture play a crucial role in maintaining collaborative relationships among parents, schools, and students. And when educators recognize and respect the cultural differences of all of the students enrolled in the school system, every individual is treated equally, regardless of race, ethnicity, language, gender, and social background. Educators need to differentiate students' cultural differences and not to see these differences as cultural deficits (Nieto, 2000, 2005). This sign of educators' respect for cultural diversity will help to fully nurture all students' identities and self-esteem. For example, Asian students represent a significant number of students enrolled in U.S. schools, especially from China, Korea, Bangladesh, and India, and it has become imperative for American educators to investigate the cultural differences of East and West and to try to understand the important role these differences play in students' learning environments and educational processes.

Figure 2.3. Cultural and Linguistic Challenges of Korean College Students in the United States

Cultural Factors	Linguistic Factors
Difficulty in openly expressing critical thinking and opinions;	Difficulties with English syntax and writing composition;
Preference for speaking Korean to other Korean classmates, and not English;	Difficulty choosing words to express intended meaning;
	Difficulty with English phonology, phonetics, and pronunciation;
Lack of class participation for fear of making mistakes;	Inability to use the correct word order to answer negative questions;
Lack of understanding of how to use and mention knowledge and information gathered from other sources;	Difficulty in understanding professors' lectures;
	Difficulty in summarizing professors' lectures;
Difficulty looking at professors in the eyes to show attention to the information presented.	

N = 19

For instance, it may be said that the American way of thinking and behaving is often direct and candid, promoting individual independence. However, Asian bilingual students, especially those recently arrived, may think and behave differently, tending to be indirect, nonexpressive, dependent, and passive. Additionally, American teachers need to understand the varying cultural norms and practices of the different subgroups (e.g., Korean students) represented under the Asian umbrella and their typical learning style because a lack of understanding can often lead to serious misinterpretation. Lee (2004) surveyed a group of Korean college students who were studying in the United States in order to identify their perceived cultural and linguistic challenges. The participants were born in Korea, had Korean as their first language, gained a high school diploma in Korea, and came to the United States to get a college degree. Figure 2.3 summarizes challenges this group mentioned as college student learners through English, their second language. The challenges they mentioned can also be applied to K–8 students confronting the English language in school for the first time.

These Korean college students found a mismatch between their linguistic and cultural styles of learning and those of the United States. For these college students, as well as for the K–12 bilingual school populations, teachers play a critical role in providing an appropriate learning environment that contributes to each student's sense of acceptance and positive self-esteem.

Academic Challenges

Many bilingual students are struggling to meet grade-level academic demands, in particular, the skills of academic English literacy (reading and writing), and the skills and knowledge of the various content areas. If students do not have the language proficiency, the literacy, and the skills to cope with grade-level curriculum, and instructional and academic standards, students struggle with the grade-level academic demands. Most of the time, bilingual students' native language development is not promoted in the classroom, and they are transferred to the mainstream English classroom with the support of only 1 or 2 hours of English as a Second Language instruction block. This lack of attention to strengthening the native language, in addition to other personal factors, may contribute to the following challenges:

- Unbalanced content area backgrounds and unfamiliar information and processes that present difficulty when learning, especially if taught in a second language (Freeman & Freeman, 2008b; Parson & Rubin, 2008).
- Increased anxiety in learning in the second language, preventing students from setting attainable learning and academic goals for themselves (August & Shanahan, 2006a; Carrasquillo & Rodríguez, 2002).
- Insufficient English academic vocabulary for expressing themselves in different academic environments (Calderón, 2007; Carrasquillo & Rodríguez, 2002; Diaz-Rico, 2008). The meaning of words and their contextual interpretation is crucial to understanding the content of oral and written texts and communication, especially the simultaneous processing of new vocabulary and the understanding of cognitively demanding concepts.
- Lack of literacy skills to keep up with the school curriculum, especially at the high school level (August & Shanahan, 2006b; Bialystok, 2001; Calderón, 2007; Carrasquillo & Rodríguez, 2002; Freeman & Freeman, 2008b; Kamil, 2003). ELLs may not have the academic proficiency required for successful completion of schoolwork, which creates difficulties when addressing literacy activities in the content areas, as well as in academic English language arts because of limited literacy skills.
- Bilingual students who do not have the opportunity to become fully literate in their primary language may not be familiar with learning strategies that promote the comprehension of complex texts (Calderón, 2007; Carrasquillo & Rodríguez, 2002; Cummins, 2005; Freeman & Freeman, 2004; Ovando & Collier, 1998). These learning strategies may include the ability to summarize a text, identify the author's purpose, infer meaning, and create a semantic map.
- Bilingual students may lack practice and experience in reading a wide range of topics at a variety of reading levels (August & Shanahan, 2006a; Smiley & Salsberry, 2007). The cognitive academic language may not have developed sufficiently to cope with the various readings and topics of the school curriculum. Due to their lack of prior knowledge, students may become frustrated when attempting to understand such a wide range of highly demanding content.

Bilingual students who have a higher level of proficiency in their first language are able to draw on that linguistic foundation during the acquisition of a new language.

USING BILINGUAL STUDENTS' NATIVE LANGUAGE IN INSTRUCTION

The educational literature uses several words to refer to the concept of "native language": *primary language, mother tongue, arterial language, ancestral language,* and *language one* (L1). All of these labels relate to the language that a person has learned and spoken from birth, usually at home and through parents or guardians. Most bilingual students are fluent speakers of their primary language before they enter school, having learned it from personal experience. The native or primary language is usually the language an individual speaks best, and it is often the basis for sociolinguistic identity. The first language is a powerful medium for communication; it has been said that it is the only language individuals can truly master on their own as long as they are surrounded by speakers of that language.

The first language is intricately bound to cognitive development and primary socialization. Echevarria and Graves (2011) see the native language as "a child's first primary tool for social interaction" (p. 40). According to Echevarria and Graves, without language, people cannot explore knowledge, exchange ideas, or expand thoughts. A conceptual framework for native language emphasis in instruction in U.S. schools includes the following two assumptions:

1. Students are more likely to learn, including the English language, if they understand what they are taught; and
2. Students with limited English proficiency will not be behind their English-speaking peers if they can keep up with subject matter content through their native language while they are learning the English language.

In 1953, the United Nations Educational, Scientific, and Cultural Organization (UNESCO) recommended the use of vernacular (native) languages in education. The report addressed the issue of which language to use with children and adults in education. The report described the physical, social, and cultural benefits of using native language instruction, as well as the many challenges faced with its implementation. UNESCO (1953) stated:

> It is axiomatic that the best medium for teaching a child is his mother tongue. Psychologically, it is the system of meaningful signs that in his mind works automatically for expression and understanding. Sociologically, it is the means of identification among the members of the community to which he belongs. Educationally, he learns more quickly through it than through an unfamiliar linguistic medium. (p. 11)

Throughout the past 6 decades, UNESCO (2003) has consistently maintained the same position on the powerful role of students' mother tongue. The organization's early and consistently repeated position on use of the students' primary/native language in school provides a guiding framework for contributing to the psychological and academic well-being of bilingual students.

Psychological Benefits

Language is a key feature of any culture and becomes an integral part of children's, youths', and adults' personalities. One's native language is the center of individual cultural and social identity. Much has been said about providing children with mental, cultural, and linguistic security, mainly acquired during their first years of native language exposure and acquisition. Acquirers who begin natural exposure to language development in childhood generally achieve higher language proficiency than those beginning as adults (Krashen, 1982). Identity formation begins the day a child is born and is nurtured when the child is welcomed and loved at home. It is the native language—the language spoken at home—that provides the child with the security and confidence to determine his or her cultural alliance, identity, and to attain self-esteem.

Advocates of bilingual education believe that a child's native language and self-esteem are tied together; ELLs bring to school a linguistic framework and foundation that is part of their emotional state when engaging in learning, especially academic reading, writing, and the acquisition of content knowledge. Nieto (2005) said that if the mother tongue of the students is not reflected in the school curriculum, it may have a negative effect on their self-esteem and cultural identity, which in turn can affect their cognitive development and achievement. When reading and writing are learned through the native language, the shock experienced and the effort put forth will feel more natural and contain less emotional trauma due to the oral foundation of the native language. For bilingual adolescents, learning content in the language that they know best becomes a less frustrating experience since these students have the oral and (often) written base of their primary language. An additional advantage of using the native language of the students in school is that the native language serves as a link between the home and the bilingual social context in which students grow up.

Linguistic Benefits

A significant percentage of bilingual students bring to school a linguistic system appropriate to their age, which includes pronunciation, vocabulary, and knowledge of the linguistic and grammatical structures of that language. These students have an age-appropriate foundation on the phonology, grammar, vocabulary, and semantics of their native language. They already have the ability and capacity to use acquired vocabulary in conversation and in other communicative activities, and through their primary language, students understand what is said to them and are able to speak and be understood. They process the written system of reading and writing, which are tied closely to their oral language. Therefore, schools can use this linguistic foundation to build academic language and introduce English as a new language. The goal is to build on all students' academic language, while giving them the language tools in both the native language and in English.

Academic Benefits

Students acquire most of their conceptual and academic knowledge and skills through the native language, which provides the foundation for completing academic tasks. Not only does the native language serve to enable students to learn the content of the curriculum, but it also serves to cultivate thinking skills. The more thinking students conduct through their strongest language, the easier and more comprehensive in their acquisition of higher-order thinking skills they will be. Academic success demands higher-level linguistic and cognitive skills, and, when these skills have been developed, students can make use of this foundation to acquire grade-level knowledge, concepts, and processes. Cognitively demanding subjects should be taught in students' primary languages, but a high level of language proficiency is needed in order to understand these subjects. This should include the study and application of cognitively demanding literacy skills.

Further, students need to be able to work with high-level concepts and abstractions. Performing school tasks successfully requires the use and comprehension of abstract and high-level academic language, what Cummins (1984) called "cognitive academic language proficiency" (CALP). Because this requires a high level of language proficiency that supports the ability to manipulate concepts, solve problems, and process complex ideas through skills such as categorizing, analyzing, and comparing, using students' strongest language in school is the most logical choice. When students demonstrate CALP, they are best able to learn the grade-level content in all subject areas, as well as master language structures and grade-level vocabulary. It has been found that when students are taught in their native language for a long period of time, they academically outperform students who are taught for a short period of time (Ramírez, Yuen, & Ramey, 1991; Thomas & Collier, 1997, 2003a).

Proficiency in a child's mother tongue is a strong predictor of second language development. Accordingly, use of one's primary language also has a positive influence on bilingual students' academic achievement (Soto, 1997; Zentella, 1997). Nieto (2005) provides an example based on interviews she conducted with successful bilingual students. She states:

> I found that maintaining language and culture were essential in supporting and sustaining academic achievement. In a series of in-depth interviews with linguistically and culturally diverse students, one of the salient features that accounted for school success was a strong-willed determination to hold onto their culture and native language. (p. 143)

Students who have a strong literacy background in their native language have been shown to develop English literacy and content knowledge faster than students who have low literacy skills (Calderón, 2007; Collier, 1987; Collier & Thomas, 2004; Echevarria & Graves, 2011). When schools promote the development of bilingual students' first language, students tend to experience academic success and develop high literacy skills in both languages.

Native language instruction not only helps to develop academic achievement in the second language in an academic setting but it also connects students' homes and community. Providing a positive learning environment with native language instruction will contribute to students' knowledge, identity, and self-confidence in becoming active members of school and the community. Researchers point to the importance of parental involvement and the home-school-community relationship in their recommendation to use the native language at home, in which children and adults are involved in creative literacy activities. Speaking, reading, and writing to children and youth in their native language promote cultural, linguistic, and academic success. This approach will foster in children positive attitudes toward their own culture and language, as well as other languages and cultures.

In 1998, the National Research Council urged literacy instruction to occur in the child's native language whenever possible. According to the council, the first language can help students in the following ways: (1) it supplies background knowledge, which makes instruction more comprehensible; and (2) it enhances the development of basic literacy.

There are individuals who believe that primary language schooling reduces bilingual students' opportunities to learn English. But authorities such as Cummins (1981), Collier (1987), and Thomas & Collier (1997, 2003a) claim that the basis of cognition and language are learned once (i.e., common underlying proficiency); thus the primary language and the second language have a shared foundation. Cummins repeatedly argues that competence in the primary language provides the foundation for competence in the second language. The Ramírez study (Ramírez, Yuen, & Ramey, 1991) provides a rationale for insisting that schools use students' native language until students have developed adequate proficiency for high-level academic work. The study recommends the implementation of late-exit bilingual programs since this type of instruction promotes the maintenance of close relationships and linguistic interactions with family members, helping students in their schoolwork and emotional needs.

We finish this section by saying that not all bilingual students demonstrate high levels of proficiency in their native language, and therefore the extent to which native language instruction translates into academic success will vary. The question educators will often ask is, Does the CALP framework serve every bilingual student? The answer is no, since in the U.S. public school system, we have several types of bilinguals. Among these are:

- Immigrant students who bring a strong native language foundation;
- Immigrant students who demonstrate many deficiencies in their native language;
- Students who were born in the United States and who are only dominant (not proficient) in the home language;
- Students who were born in the United States and who are dominant in English (mainly in the oral system) and are limited in the home language;
- Students who were born in the United States and who are "borderline" (demonstrating marginal learning behaviors), usually with limitations in both languages; and
- Students who are identified as having learning disabilities, usually with limitations in both languages.

Despite the differences of these linguistic groups, the use of the native language plays an important role in the education of all linguistically and culturally diverse students. Balderrama and Diaz-Rico (2006) summarize the importance of using the native language in the classroom with the following words:

Building on the language of the home allows students to benefit from their prior knowledge and in return bring home the knowledge they learn at school to benefit their home lives. *Replacing* the language of the home with language and experience that is disconnected from the culture of the community confuses children and leads them to under-value and distrust the home-school connection. Both building on and replacing the home language have consequences for academic achievement, cognitive development, self-esteem, and identity. (p. 94)

TEACHERS' ROLE IN THE IMPLEMENTATION OF
NATIVE LANGUAGE INSTRUCTION

One of the main factors affecting the efficiency of native language instruction is the teacher's knowledge, attitudes, and involvement regarding its implementation. Teacher beliefs about the role of native language instruction are critical to successful implementation of instruction in the classroom. Accordingly, staff development is crucial to teacher understanding of the role of the native language in the education of bilingual students. Due to the fact that many teachers have not received training in the area of native language instruction and its use in the classroom, teachers need theoretical knowledge on the subject, as well as teacher training on its implementation.

Lee (2010) conducted an open-ended pre/post survey with 38 teachers who were enrolled in an introductory course in bilingual education. The purpose of the survey was to identify teachers' beliefs and perceptions of the role of native language instruction on bilingual students' linguistic and academic development. Teachers participating in the course were given four statements to agree or disagree with, and they were also asked to write comments elaborating on their answers. In the pre-survey, only 11 teachers (28%) had a positive perception on the role of native language instruction. However, at the completion of the course 36 teachers (95%) perceived a positive role of native language. The following notion was repeated in many of the answers of the post-surveys: "In the long run, teaching non-English speakers in the native language will be beneficial in the learning of English, and it will also help them to develop academic literacy." Once teachers perceive that native language instruction is an important component in the academic development and growth of students, they incorporate effective instruction in its implementation. For example, they will use students' home and family values and beliefs as cultural supports to enhance students' academic and language development. This cultural support is reflected in teachers' incorporation of content of different cultures, traditions, and personal experiences into the curriculum. Teachers knowledgeable about bilingual programs will be motivated to use multicultural strategies to make students feel accepted and to bring other classmates into the school's cultural family. Native languages will no longer be taboo, but a regular resource and presence in the school.

Bilingual learners bring a wealth of cultural resources, both conceptual and linguistic, into the classroom. Schools, and especially teachers, need to recognize these resources as "funds of knowledge" (Moll, Amanti, Neff, & Gonzalez, 1992) and should try to incorporate them into the curriculum and school activities. Learning becomes more interesting when the teacher allows students to share their cultural histories, perspectives, and diverse viewpoints. As Skow and Stephan (2000) stated:

> In an international and multicultural classroom, students and teachers may disagree on appropriate ways of engaging in discussion, or even about whether to discuss at all. Rules of formality versus informality (e.g., raising hands to speak) or nonverbal ways of signaling confusion to the teacher (e.g., silence or inquisitive looks) are often culturally determined. (p. 355)

If these differences are well managed by the teacher, students' conversations and cooperative discussions will generate a sense of understanding and respect for differences, especially for the languages and cultures represented in the classroom. The ultimate goal is that through such understanding, the individuals involved will apply this tolerance, appreciation, and acceptance to other aspects of their lives.

BILINGUAL STUDENTS' INSTRUCTIONAL DIVERSITY

It can be said that successful programs for bilingual students take into consideration school and community culture, teacher professional development, quality of teaching, a grade-appropriate and challenging curriculum, rigorous instruction, and most important, students' needs. Whether the program includes team teaching, a theme-based curriculum, or dual-language support, instruction must be tailored to meet the diverse needs of learners from a cultural, cognitive, and emotional perspective. The following four cases of composite students represent a sampling of the different types of bilingual students in the United States and what types of programs or instruction best fit each student based on all of those considerations. While this is only a sample, these cases demonstrate the diversity of capabilities and challenges these students bring to the teaching and learning process.

As you read these cases, suppose for a moment that you are an educational consultant working in a school district in which there is a high percentage of bilingual students and a variety of instructional programs to serve the needs of this diverse school population. A school principal comes to you asking for instructional placement recommendations for four new students (a Latina, a Cambodian, a Korean, and a Russian), registered at the school. The principal, who recognizes you as a knowledgeable and experienced educator, wants to consult with you on the best instructional placement for these four students. The principal asks you the following three questions: (1) What is the "right program" for these students? (2) What type of curriculum should be offered to these students?; and (3) How or to what extent can the school use the cognitive, academic, and linguistic foundations these students bring? Brief overviews of each student and placement recommendations for each student follow.

Student 1: María Elena

María Elena was born in Flagstaff, Arizona, to Mexican immigrant parents. Both parents work 7 days a week and leave María Elena to the care of her grandmother. Since 1st grade, María Elena has been enrolled in a transitional bilingual program where she has been taught most of the content areas in Spanish with the support of an ESL program, providing conversation, vocabulary, grammar, and basic readings skills. Now she is in 3rd grade, and her parents have moved to another state. The grandmother came to the school to enroll her and left with the hope that María Elena would continue to use Spanish in school and continue to develop and grow in her mastery of English.

Programmatic and Instructional Recommendations

It is recommended that María Elena be enrolled in a transitional bilingual program; luckily, this new school has such a program. She will continue to be taught primarily in the home language until she becomes proficient in English and is able to perform academically well in a mainstream classroom. As María Elena becomes more proficient in English, instruction in the native language may decrease. Fortunately, María Elena's grandmother is pleased to continue to promote the native language through reading and to attend a community-based after-school program for further development of Spanish literacy.

Student 2: Raska

Raska was born and raised in Phnom Penh, Cambodia. She is the eldest of five children. Raska attended school for 3½ years in Cambodia, but she had to quit to stay home and take care of her siblings. During those few school years, she acquired a basic level of literacy in Mon-Khmer. When she was 14, her family relocated to a refugee camp in San Diego where Raska attended English language classes and learned interpersonal English language skills, as well as basic reading (mainly decoding) and writing in English. Two years later, she enrolled in high school, where she was struggling with English academic language, especially in the different content areas. She felt frustrated and refused to continue in the school. The school district agreed to transfer her to a new school.

Programmatic and Instructional Recommendations

A content-based ESL program may be the best instructional approach for Raska. In this program, content will be made comprehensible through sheltered instruction (simplification of language, nonverbal communication, visual aids, simple grammatical structures, repetition, summaries, and continuous checking for understanding) as well as using native language resources including, for instance, cognates, cultural content, and multicultural literature. Eventually, when Raska becomes more comfortable with the English language and instruction, more academic language will be gradually incorporated. Cambodian culture will be presented in the curriculum. Raska's prior knowledge is recognized and used to drive instruction.

Student 3: Chang Woo

Chang Woo was born and educated in Seoul until the 2nd grade when he came to Los Angeles at the age of 9. He spoke Korean at home. His father received a master's degree in business from the United States and decided to stay and work in the financial district, bringing his family to the United States along with him. Chang Woo had been a good student at school in South Korea and studied English as a foreign language from the 1st grade. His father wants Chang Woo to continue using the Korean language and to enroll his son in a new school with the hope of receiving instruction in English and Korean.

Programmatic and Instructional Recommendations

Chang Woo would thrive in a dual-bilingual-language program where he would achieve high levels of proficiency in English and Korean, biliteracy (reading and writing in the two languages), and cross-cultural understanding. The dual-language program integrates language and content so that Chang Woo will develop high language proficiency levels, academic content knowledge, as well as grade-level achievement. It would be explained to the parents that these optimal outcomes will not be seen immediately. However, by being persistent and supporting the school with cultural and language resources, Chang Woo will likely outperform many other students, including native English speakers.

Student 4: Ahtoh

Ahtoh came to New York City when she was 6½ years old. She attended kindergarten in Russia, and when she left Russia, she had, for her age, a strong oral command of the Russian language. She had also learned to decode and to write 15 to 20 simple words. She is ready to go to the 1st grade in the New York City public school district. Her parents want to place her in a Russian/English developmental bilingual program. They want her to be able to learn English, but at the same time want the school to recognize and support Athoh's native culture and language.

Programmatic and Instructional Recommendations

The developmental bilingual program is recommended for Ahtoh. This program will best meet the immediate academic needs of Ahtoh because her proficiency level in the native language is strong for her age. Her instructional program will consist of an extended native language component with a strong English as a Second Language component. Initially, Ahtoh will learn to read in Russian, learn mathematics, science, and social studies in Russian, and will begin to use English for communication purposes, especially to communicate with and be understood by teachers and peers. Main components of the instructional program are the acquisition of vocabulary; the expansion of concepts acquired in the primary language; and use of the Russian culture as part of the curriculum content. Her parents play an important role in using Athoh's primary language in her overall language and literacy development. Ahtoh's parents must encourage Ahtoh to be surrounded by books in Russian and in English.

PARENTS AS RESOURCES

Parents are valuable resources for schools and for their own children. It is critical that schools use community members and family members to share their experiences with students, teachers, and other school personnel in order to form and maintain successful parent-school relationships. Ovando & Collier (1998) contend that parent involvement is a key factor that influences the academic achievement of students and the development of school attitudes conducive to teaching diverse learners. In general, parent involvement in schools positively affects children's achievement, more so in reading and writing development. We strongly recommend that schools try at least the following activities to engage parents as partners, making them active and accountable:

1. Invite parents to share their personal experiences and family cultures in their children's school. By inviting community members and family members to share their expertise or experiences with the school personnel, whether in a classroom or other school location, educators provide parents with an opportunity to become active participants in the school community.

2. Invite parents to share their heritage through the celebration of holidays and themes throughout the year. Teachers ask parents to come and present a variety of cultural activities, such as reading a book about their country, providing hands-on activities by demonstrating a craft or technique from their own culture, and being in the classroom to celebrate and share a holiday with students. These holidays might include the celebration of the Lunar/Chinese New Year, Valentine's Day, St. Patrick's Day, Diwali, Hanukkah, or Kwanzaa. When parents participate in the celebration of ethnically diverse holidays, bilingual students have a unique opportunity to engage with different ethnic groups in celebration. This is one more opportunity for students to emphasize and see similarities that may render differences superficial. It has become increasingly apparent that a lack of understanding and appreciation of differences can lead to significant discord and alienation rather than unity (Chu, 1993).

3. Organize family literacy projects. One example of a family literacy project is to guide parents to ask their children to tell a story. Then, the parents write another story and read it to the children. In this way, parents and children can share their experiences together and appreciate their own culture together (Diaz-Rico, 2008). Other literacy projects may include (a) development of a "community book" at home; (b) preparation of a cultural almanac identifying the most important dates of their own culture; (c) writing a journal about a specific topic (e.g., the care of a home pet); and (d) a collection of songs from their native country. These activities should be prepared in the families' strongest language.

RESOURCE MATERIALS

There are many resources that educators, specifically teachers, can use to implement native language instruction. The following is a sampling of the many tools that are currently available in facilitating teachers' implementation of native language instruction.

1. Classroom library: This is an excellent resource that provides students with access to texts on a daily basis. Educators can include in their libraries content from students' languages and cultures. Books may include stories presented in several languages, dictionaries, nonfiction, and audiobooks. It can also include the same story in different languages (e.g., Cinderella).

2. School library. Keeping multicultural and native language literature in the library shows students that their language and culture are accepted and welcomed in the school. The librarian and teachers should work together to develop projects throughout the year to use these books in research or special projects.

3. Cultural field trips. Taking students to different historic and ethnic places, such as museums, ethnic restaurants, and historical centers, provides students with an additional opportunity to strengthen their native language and further develop their own cultural tolerance and understanding.

3

Teaching Language Arts Using Bilingual Students' Native Language

I am a Spanish speaking immigrant,
switching from "What's up?" to "¿Qué pasa brother?"
able to speak in English with my face and hands
thinking in Spanish and drafting in English.
I play many roles at home: translator for mami
at the doctor's office, at the bank and the post office
answering questions, passing on information.
I am the care taker for my sister Lupe
waiting at school to walk her home
providing her a snack before the homework.
I read the mail my two abuelos *receive.*
I help papi *in assembling furniture,*
Spanish and English; helping me both.

(Angela Carrasquillo, "I Am an Immigrant Student")

Language arts is the subject area of the school curriculum that provides students with instructional experiences to develop proficiency in the acquisition, development, and mastery of the art of listening, speaking, reading, and writing. Bilingual students in the United States who are enrolled in a bilingual program usually receive two sections daily of language arts, one in English, and one in their native language. In this chapter, we address the role of the bilingual students' language arts in the native language to promote students' language and literacy development. The chapter provides answers to the following questions: (1) What steps are followed by schools to identify the appropriate language arts program for bilingual students?; (2) What should be the main areas of emphasis in implementing the native language arts curriculum?; (3) What instructional strategies are recommended to enhance bilingual students' native language?; and (4) Which writing modes and tasks contribute to bilingual students' success in writing?

IDENTIFYING THE APPROPRIATE LANGUAGE ARTS PROGRAM FOR BILINGUAL STUDENTS

Many English learners in K–12 schools were born in the United States: three-fourths of the identified English language learners at the elementary school level are native born, and more than half of the secondary English language learners are native born

(Carrasquillo & Rodríguez, 2002). Approximately 40% of elementary and secondary bilingual students speak a language other than English at home. This means there are a significant number of students who were born outside of the United States, and they represent more than 100 different language groups. Due to this linguistic diversity, it is extremely important to determine a student's appropriate language arts program for instruction. Across all grades K–12, the following questions are critical when seeking to identify the language(s) for instruction: What is their native/primary language? Is English their first language, or is it their heritage/home language? What is the language spoken at home? What early childhood linguistic experiences did learners have in the native language as well as in the second?

In most cases, schools and school districts in the United States develop steps and procedures to identify bilingual students' language proficiency, especially in English. The administration uses the language assessment information to place students in appropriate instructional programs and services. Although, in the majority of cases, language identification procedures are mainly used to identify students' levels of English language proficiency, the acquired information is also useful for determining the appropriate instructional placement type (e.g., bilingual program, free standing/pull-out/pull-in English as a Second Language program, or an English-only mainstream program). A quick search of procedures used in U.S. schools or school districts shows that there are three main procedures used within school districts to determine bilingual students' strongest language for instruction: (1) getting information about students' home language characteristics and literacy background through a *Home Language Survey/Questionnaire*; (2) finding information on students' dominant language and language characteristics by using an interview or a set of observations; and (3) using language proficiency assessment tests to determine students' level of language competence. Figure 3.1 provides a list of the procedures that are used in the five states with the largest enrollments of bilingual students learning English in the United States.

Home Language Characteristics and Literacy Background

Under federal and state law, schools are responsible for using assessment tools to identify new students' home language characteristics. Most states have developed tools to identify this information in a format of a *Home Language Survey* (HLS) or a *Home Language Questionnaire* (HLQ), which is typically used first to identify whether the new student speaks a language other than English at home. The questionnaire is often available in several languages, but when that is not the case the items can be translated into the student's home language. Usually, this questionnaire is completed by the child's parent or guardian. If the responses on the questionnaire indicate that the student is speaking and using a language other than English, the school's next step is to follow up with an interview and an assessment proficiency test.

States do not have to use the exact survey format as long as the one developed and approved provides the required information on students' home language characteristics. Figure 3.2 presents a fragment of the *Home Language Questionnaire* in place at the New York State Department of Education, in a state with a bilingual/English learners' enrollment of more than 200,000 (New York State Education Department, 2011).

Figure 3.1. Procedures for English Language Learners' Language Identification

State	Home Language Information	Student's Interview	Assessment Tests
Arizona	*Home Language Survey:* Identifies the primary language used at home; the language most often spoken by the student; and the first language spoken.	It is not state mandated.	*Oral English Language Proficiency Test (grades K–1).* *Oral, Reading, and Writing English Proficiency Tests (grades 2–12).*
California	*Home Language Survey:* Identifies the primary language used in the home; the language most often spoken by the student; the language often spoken by adults at home; and the language first acquired.	It is not state mandated.	*California English Language Development Test* (CELDT) *Informal Assessment of Primary Language Proficiency.*
Florida	*Home Language Survey:* Identifies the primary language used at home; the language most often spoken by the student; and the language that the student first acquired.	It is not state mandated.	*Language Assessment Battery-Revised (grades K–12).*
New York	*Home Language Questionnaire:* Identifies the primary language used at home; the language most often spoken by the student; and the language that the student first acquired.	Interview is conducted in English and the native language to identify student's understanding of English.	*Language Assessment Battery–Revised* (LAB-R)
Texas	*Home Language Survey:* Identifies the primary language used in the home and the language most often spoken by the student.	It is not state mandated.	*Oral Language Proficiency Test* (grades Pre-K–1) *Oral Language Proficiency Test and English Reading and English Language Arts* (grades 2–12).

Informal Student Interview

Once a bilingual student's home language characteristics and literacy background have been identified, some states (such as New York) recommend an informal student interview in both languages for the purpose of a "preliminary assessment of a student's understanding of, and ability to speak the English language" (New York State Education Department, 2011, p. 3). If the interview indicates that the student is able to answer all the questions in English and if the HLS reveals that he or she speaks English, the identification process is stopped, and the student is placed in a general education or mainstream program. Unfortunately, these interviews are often conducted to get additional information on a student's English characteristics, and not necessarily on native language characteristics. Consequently, this procedure may indicate a lost opportunity because the interview should be used for both identification of English and native language competence and dominance.

Figure 3.2 Home Language Questionnaire (HLQ)- Korean and English

THE STATE EDUCATION DEPARTMENT / THE UNIVERSITY OF THE STATE OF NEW YORK
ALBANY, NEW YORK 12234
뉴욕주교육부

Home Language Questionnaire(HLQ) - KOREAN
가 정 언 어 설 문 지

교직원작성란(To be completed by school personnel)	
학군(District)	(정자기입)
학교(School)	학년(Grade)
학생이름(Student Name)	
생년월일(Date of Birth) 월(Month) 일(Day) 년(Year)	
학생고유번호(Student Identification Number)	
출생국/모국(Country of Birth/Ancestry)	
미국 외에서 교육받은 햇수(Number of years enrolled in school outside the U.S.)	
작성자의 이름과 직위(Name/Position of School Personnel Completing This Section)	
판정(Determination)	☐LEP 가능성(Possible LEP) ☐영어능숙(English Proficient)

친애하는 학부모 또는 보호자님께

위댁의 자녀에게 가장 적절한 교육을 제공하기 위해, 학생이 영어를 얼마나 잘 이해하고, 말하고, 읽고, 쓰는지를 알아야 할 필요가 있습니다.

이 설문지 작성에 협조해 주시면 감사하겠습니다.

감사합니다.

(해당사항에 ✓로 하시오)

1. 학생의 가정에서 사용하는 언어(들)은 무엇입니까?　☐ 영어　☐ 기타＿＿＿＿＿＿
구체적으로 기입하십시오

2. 가정에서 학생에게 말할때 주로 사용하는 언어(들)은 무엇입니까?　☐ 영어　☐ 기타＿＿＿＿＿＿
구체적으로 기입하십시오

3. 학생이 듣고 이해하는 언어(들)은 무엇입니까?　☐ 영어　☐ 기타＿＿＿＿＿＿
구체적으로 기입하십시오

4. 학생이 말할때 사용하는 언어(들)은 무엇입니까?　☐ 영어　☐ 기타＿＿＿＿＿＿
구체적으로 기입하십시오

5. 학생이 읽을 줄 아는 언어(들)은 무엇입니까?　☐ 영어　☐ 기타＿＿＿＿＿　☐ 읽지 못함
구체적으로 기입하십시오

6. 학생이 쓸때 사용하는 언어(들)은 무엇입니까?　☐ 영어　☐ 기타＿＿＿＿＿　☐ 쓰지 못함
구체적으로 기입하십시오

7. 귀하의 의견으로는 학생이 영어를 얼마나 잘 이해하고, 말하고, 읽고, 쓴다고 생각하십니까?

	아주잘함	조금함	전혀못함
영어로 듣고 이해하기	☐	☐	☐
영어로 말하기	☐	☐	☐
영어로 읽기	☐	☐	☐
영어로 쓰기	☐	☐	☐

	월(Month)	일(Day)	년(Year)

부모 또는 보호지의 서명(Signature of Parent/Guardian/Other)　날짜(Date)

The University of the State of New York • The State Education Department • Office of Bilingual Education
Albany, New York 12234

Home Language Questionnaire (HLQ)

Dear Parent or Guardian:

In order to provide your child with the best possible education, we need to determine how well he or she understands, speaks, reads and writes English. Your assistance in answering these questions is greatly appreciated.

Thank You

(✔ boxes that apply)

1. What language(s) is spoken in the student's home or residence? ❏ English ❏ Other _____ *specify*

2. What language(s) are spoken most of the time to the student, in the home or residence? ❏ English ❏ Other _____ *specify*

3. What language(s) does the student understand? ❏ English ❏ Other _____ *specify*

4. What language(s) does the student speak? ❏ English ❏ Other _____ *specify*

5. What language(s) does the student read? ❏ English ❏ Other _____ *specify* ❏ Does Not Read

6. What language(s) does the student write? ❏ English ❏ Other _____ *specify* ❏ Does Not Write

7. In your opinion, how well does the student understand, speak, read and write English?

	Very well	Only a little	Not at all
Understands English	❏	❏	❏
Speaks English	❏	❏	❏
Reads English	❏	❏	❏
Writes English	❏	❏	❏

	Month:	Day:	Year:

Signature of Parent/Guardian/Other   Date   HLQ (2/00) 99:337 PM

Source: New York State Education Department, Office of Bilingual Education and Foreign Language Studies.

Identification of Students' Language Proficiency

Although the HLS helps educators identify bilingual students' primary language and home language characteristics, further language assessment is needed to verify the information collected by the two informal assessment tools. Most states provide language assessment tests for English learners. For example, in New York State, students are assessed using the *Language Assessment Battery-Revised* (LAB-R). The LAB-R consists of three sections—listening, reading, and writing—and it is administered as an initial screening tool upon a student's enrollment in a New York public school for the first time. The LAB-R results determine the placement of the student, which may be in a bilingual, or English as a Second Language (ESL) program, or in mainstream general education. In California, the *California English Language Development Test* (CELDT) is used as an initial language assessment for K–12 students learning English and as an annual assessment of language progress. The CELDT includes four sections: listening, speaking, reading, and writing. The California Department of Education (2011) states that the purpose of this test is to identify a student's level of English proficiency and his or her progress over time. California also uses the *Informal Assessment of Primary Language Proficiency,* which provides additional information on students' prior school experiences, and native oral language and literacy skills (reading and writing).

Although several state education departments provide the HLS in a diversity of languages, most states use language proficiency tests to measure English proficiency. California and New York administer proficiency tests in Spanish.

Parental Involvement in Identifying the Appropriate Instructional Program for Their Children

In most school districts in the United States, it is the school's responsibility to notify the parents of the results of their children's assessments, and to recommend an appropriate instructional program for their children. Parents may opt to enroll their children in a bilingual program, in an English as a Second Language program, or in the school's English-only mainstream program with or without specialized English language assistance.

In bilingual programs, students are provided with appropriate instruction to become proficient in English and to use the native language for the advancement and enrichment of literacy and the acquisition of content knowledge, processes, and skills. The assumption is that students' home languages develop when they are "cultivated, encouraged, and promoted in a purposeful way in many or all curriculum areas" (Baker, 2006, p. 204). If the recommended program is a bilingual one, it must have a well-planned and implemented native language component.

THE NATIVE LANGUAGE ARTS CURRICULUM: LEARNING STANDARDS AND EXPECTATIONS

Language arts as a school subject area is conceptualized as a deliberate curriculum that includes the development of students' listening, speaking, reading, and writing skills and processes through a prescribed set of language and literacy experiences in order to

**Figure 3.3. The Common Core State Standards
Language Arts Curriculum Focus**

Speaking/Listening	• Meaningful oral communication, • Interpersonal (collaborative communication), • Adaptation of speech to context and task, • Vocabulary meaning and relationships.
Reading	• Reading complex informational texts independently in a variety of areas, • Balancing between literature and informational texts (including science, history, technical documents, etc.).
Writing	Writing for different purposes: • to summarize, • to explain, • to describe, • to persuade/opinions.

Source: National Government Association Center for Best Practices & Council of Chief State School Officers, 2010a.

prepare them to become lifelong literate and academically successful adults and citizens. The current language arts curriculum in many schools has been greatly influenced by the standards-based education reform movement in the United States regarding educating public school students, which is the idea of developing a set of "common learning outcomes," expectations, or "standards" that are basic and necessary to all students and measured through standardized grade-level assessments. Learning standards are statements that express what students ought to know or what they should be capable of doing at particular points in their learning progression. A complete set of standards is directed toward the attainment of a general goal, and these standards are used by schools to guide instruction. The language arts curriculum must follow grade-level goals/standards, which identify expectations for attaining particular knowledge and capabilities in language arts courses (National Government Association Center for Best Practices & Council of Chief State School Officers, 2010a). These language and literacy expectations are often called "learning standards." The emphasis for the language arts curriculum is on literacy learning across the curriculum, focusing on cognitive skills such as problem formulation, research investigation, and interpretation of communication. Figure 3.3 provides a summary of the language arts curriculum based on the Common Core State Standards (CCSS).

School principals and teachers agree that learning standards do not dictate the content of the language arts instruction; its focus and purpose are meant to be used as a guide in the development of learning experiences. For example, learning standards guide bilingual teachers as they plan to instruct bilingual students in first or second language. The National Government Association Center for Best Practices & Council of Chief State School Officers (2010b) in identifying the application of the *Common Core State Standards* (CCSS) for ELLs stated the need for rigorous grade-level expectations in the areas of speaking, listening, reading, and writing to prepare all students to be college and career ready, including English language learners. Second-language learners also will benefit from instruction about how to negotiate situations outside of those settings so they are able to participate on equal footing with native speakers in all aspects of social, economic, and civic endeavors. (p. 1)

The organization also stated, "ELLs who are literate in a first language that shares cognates with English can apply first-language vocabulary knowledge when reading in English; likewise ELLs with high levels of schooling can often bring to bear conceptual knowledge developed in their first knowledge when reading in English" (p. 1). Although the CCSS see the native language as an additive factor in English language acquisition and development, and not as an enhancement of the students' native language in itself, it clearly identifies the importance of native language literacy and background knowledge in bilingual students' learning and academic development. Teachers should have these standards in mind when planning instruction for the development of language and literacy. These sets of learning expectations guide language arts in English and language arts in the native language. When language arts instruction is provided in the first language, attention is given to the student's facility with his or her primary language as well as the content to use, to allow for the inclusion of students' prior knowledge, cultural content, and perspectives.

In addition to the general expectations required in the area of language and literacy, there is a set of expectations related to students' grade-level achievement. Figure 3.4 shows teachers' academic expectations, based on the CCSS for language arts and curriculum.

Figure 3.5 provides examples of instructional activities illustrating how to implement the language arts curriculum in the native language following the CCSS.

The native language grade-level curriculum is designed to help bilingual students become independent learners. In practical terms, independent learners master the language and content sufficiently, which enables them to

- Comprehend and evaluate texts;
- Construct effective arguments;
- Ask relevant questions;
- Listen and respond;
- Demonstrate command of the oral language;
- Use a wide range of grade-level vocabulary;
- Use resources to assist in learning; and
- Demonstrate learning though a variety of individual products.

Figure 3.6 illustrates steps to follow in the implementation of a native language arts lesson.

Figure 3.4. Academic Expectations Within the Language Arts Curriculum

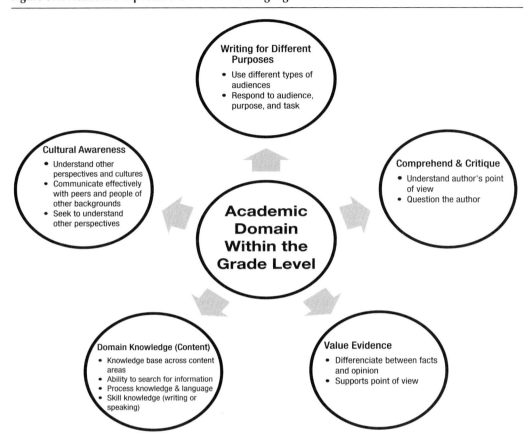

Figure 3.5. Native Language Arts Instructional Activities Focusing on Common Core State Standards

English Language Arts Curriculum Domains	Instructional Activities	Student Products
Knowledge	Display a video clip outlining the content that needs to be covered.	Identify the main ideas of the content.
Cultural Awareness	Discussion of information from supermarket circulars comparing ethnic products.	Prepare a list of foods and explain how the food is prepared in different countries.
Value Evidence	Identification of facts and opinions of a text.	Write a persuasive letter to the author expressing the student's perspectives.
Reading Comprehension	Analysis of an essay providing author's point of view to persuade readers.	Write of a retelling or reading response to the essay.
Response to Audience	Role-play a debate on the "colonial time" topic of "taxation without representation."	Write an expository essay using the student's point of view on "taxation without representation."
Writing for Different Purposes	Small groups' discussion on the advantages and disadvantages of technology.	Write an argumentative essay on the effects of technology (positive and negative).

Figure 3.6. Steps for Developing Native Language Arts Lessons

Step 1: Identify the grade-level English language arts learning standards. Include listening, speaking, reading, and writing skills and processes.

Step 2: Examine level of native language proficiency of the students to identify appropriate instructional content for attainment of the learning outcomes.

Step 3: Identify culturally relevant content to meet the content language needs and interests of the students.

- Examine types of reading (e.g., narrative, expository)
- Examine the length of the reading (to eliminate unnecessary information, which may diminish learner confidence)
- Identify a short list of key words: "Why are those words important?" "What language and literacy skills can be developed by knowing the meaning and function of the words?"

Step 4: Identify specific instructional strategies and activities to address the learning standards.

Step 5: At the beginning of the lesson, use an intriguing activity to create interest in the content to be learned.

- Introduce terms and concepts that are necessary to understand the lesson.
- Use scaffolding strategies (e.g., charts, visuals, word maps) to help learners understand concepts and structures.

Step 6: Engage students in conversations and activities throughout the lesson in order to maintain interest:

- Elicit comprehension questions related to the key questions.
- Ask students to repeat the question.
- Continue to ask questions such as "What should you do if you do not understand the question?"
- Rehearse steps to enhance listening comprehension.
- Ask students to repeat other classmates' answers to practice listening, speaking, and comprehension.

Step 7: Engage students in reading the text to answer one or two main questions. In early grades, teachers can do oral reading; in the more advanced grades, silent reading usually fosters more concentration.

- Students can read the entire text, or the reading text may be divided into sections, depending on students' reading proficiencies.
- Provide students plenty of opportunities to attain the skills identified in the lesson objectives and targets (e.g., main ideas, details to support main ideas, comparing fact with opinion, questioning the author).

Step 8: Based on the identified learning standards, choose one or two main assessment strategies in order to determine students' understanding of the lesson, and the level of acquisition of the particular skills developed through the lesson. Here are some examples:

- Debrief with the whole class about content and skills.
- Require students to write statements in reply to particular questions (e.g., "What did you learn from this lesson/story?")
- Recommend or require students to write the author a letter to gain additional insights into various issues.

ENHANCING STUDENTS' ORAL LANGUAGE FOUNDATION

By using the native language in the language arts classroom students are able to use the linguistic and cognitive foundation they have for gaining more sophisticated linguistic knowledge as well as conceptual and content knowledge. Language is an integration of four processes: listening, speaking, reading, and writing. These four linguistic processes, although independent, are interrelated, and work in conjunction with the cognitive processes of learning. By enhancing students' oral native language foundation, teachers are also building concepts, vocabulary, and linguistic structures for literacy development (Goldenberg, 2008). Students, especially those who are bilingual, bring an oral foundation upon which they build language understanding to meet the demands of increasingly complex content, which requires learners to increase their processing skills in order to listen for understanding and to speak for communication. Good listeners use an array of cognitive strategies (Dunkel, 1986) to obtain meaning from what they hear, (sort out what they hear and what they need to know; predict some of the information; decide on how much of the information is relevant; and check for understanding of the message). In addition, speaking allows individuals to express themselves concisely, coherently, and in a manner that suits all audiences and occasions (Carrasquillo & Rodríguez, 2002). Teachers need to provide an environment to enhance the oral language foundation that students bring to the classroom. This will help them advance in communication and oral comprehensibility, enabling them to become communicative and confident users of their native language for whatever purposes they need.

In the native language classroom, teachers should accept and build on the oral language foundation students bring, and then scaffold a temporary support for learning, which is used to help the students construct knowledge. Scaffolding strategies may include focusing learner attention on one specific task, dividing a task into smaller subcomponents, using representational formats, using a variety of learning modes, using graphic organizers, and using thinking strategies. The development of oral academic language is based on the following premises: (1) communication is meaningful and interesting to students; (2) students are challenged to become involved; (3) instructional context provides opportunities to develop vocabulary and concept formation; and, (4) instruction is contextualized and learners practice continuously.

THE DEVELOPMENT OF READING COMPREHENSION IN THE NATIVE LANGUAGE

Reading is the process of constructing meaning through the dynamic interaction among the reader's existing knowledge, the information conveyed by the language, and the context of the reading situation (Weaver, 1988). The process of understanding a text is a function of the interaction between the written words and how they trigger the reader's knowledge. When reading, individuals actively and continually engage in use of language knowledge, world knowledge, and understanding of print conventions to make sense of the written text and to engage in an active interaction process to understand the meaning of the text. Readers need to be actively involved in their reading and interested in the content being read.

The purpose of reading significantly influences the strategies learners use and how much they remember of what they read. Accordingly, educators need to be aware of students' linguistic knowledge, home, and community language, as well as cultural background, to provide content that is relevant and interesting. Comprehension will take place only when the information in the text triggers a response from readers whose background knowledge has been activated. Students who lack background knowledge about the content presented may only be able to make superficial predictions or inferences about what they read.

It is well established that reading comprehension is the backbone of making students literate. What do educators know about the teaching of reading comprehension in school? Educators know that

- Reading comprehension is influenced by prior domain knowledge, cognitive reading strategies, and decoding fluency and phonemic awareness;
- Students' prior domain knowledge is a prediction of student ability to comprehend or to learn from texts;
- The enhancement of domain knowledge needs to be fostered along with comprehension strategies;
- Teaching students how to use reading strategies can enhance their reading comprehension;
- Initially, teachers need to spend sufficient time on building background for reading (as well as for writing) plus create mental schemes in organizing content and conceptual structures; and
- The number of reading strategies students use to become competent readers is relatively small and can be taught, for instance, by making connections between the text and prior knowledge of the learners; making inferences to connect information; visualizing and creating mental images; and asking questions throughout the reading.

Teachers need to promote reading comprehension by encouraging, expecting, and requiring students to read a diversity of texts in the native language (informational, fictional, historical, scientific, and technical) for a variety of purposes as recommended by the CCSS regarding text complexity and range of reading. Students who have been guided to read diverse texts are better able to read complex texts, especially those readings that include difficult levels of meaning, vocabulary, structure, syntax, and language. What are the levels of reading comprehension needed? We go back to Bloom's taxonomy (1956) and Anderson and Krathwohl's (2000) reconceptualization to identify the levels of cognitive domains required to read complex texts.

Because students must be able to independently and proficiently read and comprehend a diversity of complex texts in and out of school, teachers should use different reading strategies to guide students to comprehend the dimensions of the different texts. Two strategies, namely reciprocal teaching and jigsaw reading groups, are recommended to help students get meaning from written texts, especially those of an informational nature.

Reciprocal Teaching

In this strategy, students become the teacher and lead communicative activities regarding content presented in a written text (literature or informational). For example, after students read the text silently, students may become teachers for small groups of students and ask questions about main points or details presented in the text. It is important that the students acting as teachers should think critically about responses to their questions. This activity is very effective in the native language classroom creating a nonthreatening atmosphere where students can share information without being afraid of making oral mistakes.

Jigsaw Reading Group

For this strategy, the class is divided into small groups and each member of the groups is given a separate task to help in the understanding of the meaning of a written text (e.g., identification of the two main characters of the story, underlining the main points presented in the information). Each individual has a special role and is responsible for learning a part of the text and sharing it with a member of another group. To do this, members of other groups who share the same task meet in temporary "expert" groups to discuss what they have learned. After that, the whole class comes together to discuss the content of the text and what was learned.

THE ROLE OF VOCABULARY IN ENHANCING READING COMPREHENSION

Vocabulary knowledge is vital for expressing one's self and plays a crucial role in students' academic preparation. Because the meaning of words is crucial to understanding the content of oral messages and written texts, progressively building vocabulary enables learners to master increasingly complex content taught in school. The more sophisticated students' vocabulary is, the better their comprehension will be.

Students bring a core of vocabulary in the first language that needs to be expanded before, during, and after lessons, especially in the language arts classroom. Due to the diversity of students represented in the native language classroom, vocabulary and background building are essential components in expanding students' literacy development, especially for reading comprehension and grade-level writing. High frequency of unfamiliar words in a text presents a dimension of difficulty in understanding the main ideas. Literate individuals are able to determine word meanings, identify the nuances of words, and to expand their repertoire of words and phrases, particularly those important to academic discourse. Students will develop their vocabularies through a mix of conversations, direct instruction, independent reading, and experiences.

We recommend the explicit teaching of vocabulary, not only for reading but also for listening, self-expression, and writing. Emphasis on vocabulary building must be present in daily instruction, and needs to be constantly used for students' acquisition and mastery. There are instructional strategies geared at enhancing students' vocabulary. The following three recommendations are useful for building students' vocabulary in the native language arts classroom.

1. Build vocabulary through the provision of background knowledge on the topic. The presentation of an isolated vocabulary list does not always produce comprehension of the concepts behind the labels. The assumption is that the lack of background knowledge, which is often academically based, negatively impacts the vocabulary background related to the topic. Pre-lesson conversations and activities addressing key vocabulary of the lesson support efficient understanding and comprehension of the lesson.

2. Vocabulary acquisition and development is most effective when it is appropriately contextualized, that is, taught in contexts that are natural, functional, and of immediate interest and use. The most effective vocabulary development takes place in lessons that address conceptual information. The linguistic and conceptual contexts of the lesson are likely to be effective when they contain diverse areas of interest and relevant purposes. In addition, students need to become familiar with functional use of technological resources such as the Internet to utilize online dictionaries, thesauri, and encyclopedias.

3. There are scaffolding strategies that help students visualize the meaning and function of new words. Semantic mapping and advance graphic organizers are two recommended strategies. A semantic map shows relationships in ways that appeal to and make sense to visual learners. Also, as the map or web grows and interrelates, students can see the conceptual relationships and develop fuller understanding of word families or categories and how they function as guides to information and meaning. The advance organizer strategy provides opportunities to activate students' prior knowledge as well as introduce key vocabulary. For example, some stories or literature selections provide a brief summary, often on the back of the book or at the beginning of a short story. Usually, it includes a question or comment designed to entice the reader into reading the selection. Teachers can use these summaries to interest their students in the story, to activate background knowledge, and to introduce key or new vocabulary.

MULTICULTURAL LITERATURE

Using literature in classrooms enhances students' language and literacy, and it provides readers with opportunities to think and react about text (Amour, 2003; Goldenberg, 2008; Walker-Dalhouse, 2008). Literature fosters the imagination by presenting a range of characters, ideas, and information. It is a great tool to introduce students to literacy and to expand their knowledge base. In the native language arts classroom, students need to read books originally written in the native language, chosen by the teacher, and directed by curriculum guidelines, but students also need to read books of their own choosing. The students should be provided with sustained time for both independent reading and collaborative book sharing, including discussions between students and teachers (Balderrama & Diaz-Rico, 2006). Through the analysis of literature, students meet a diversity of characters; are exposed to different perspectives; are able to become familiar with different types of authors; compare authors' points of view on a similar topic; express their opinions; and become lifelong successful readers. Tompkins (2001) stated, "Literature also helps children understand how the institutions of society and the forces of nature affect them. Through reading, students learn about the power of language to narrate a story or to persuade. Literature is our cultural heritage and should be central to our curriculum" (p. 29). Multicultural literature should be encouraged in the native language arts classroom; it is an important venue for preserving, recording, and revealing culture and it encourages social interaction between authors and readers.

In native language arts classrooms, teachers have more flexibility in choosing readings to match students' language proficiency level, ethnic backgrounds, and age and gender interests. Teachers need to provide a selection of reading texts or reading selections that include all or most of the following types of literature:

- Readings with adapted vocabulary and length as provided in curriculum-based reading series;
- Reading series, including a variety of topics, reading levels, and text structures (e.g., *Big Books*);
- Thematic readings, including age-related topics or multicultural ethnic themes;
- Core books that are mainly identified by the school, the district, or state education departments (e.g., adopted list);
- Readers grouped by an integrated theme, usually involving the presentation of a topic from different perspectives (e.g., flora in deserts); and
- Self-selected books for independent reading.

We strongly recommend the inclusion of multicultural literature. Culture plays an important role in an individual's formation. Including multicultural books in the curriculum is a good strategy to close the gap between the culture of the school and that of the home. Literature that presents the cultural contributions and lifestyles of various ethnic groups helps students get a better understanding of themselves and allows them to see their own culture represented in the school curriculum.

There are many organizations and groups involved in the compilation and dissemination of books representing different cultures:

1. Shen's Books is a publisher of multicultural children's literature that emphasizes cultural diversity and affirming differences. The books focus on introducing children to the cultures of Asia (China, Japan, Southwest Asia, India, Pacific Islands) with the purpose of sharing a world of stories, and building greater understanding and affirming identities within increasingly diverse communities. For example, the book *Cinderella* has its own Filipino, Cambodian, and Hmong versions.
2. Day Books is an independent publishing company that distributes diaries from around the world.
3. The Council on Interracial Books for Children is a nonprofit organization whose main role is the promotion and development of children's literature that adequately reflects the multicultural society.
4. Hispanic Heritage Booklist is a recommended list of children's books by Hispanic and Latin American children's authors. It was compiled by the Colorín Colorado organization.

5. Doorways to Culture and Tradition (Seattle Public Library) is a recommended list of Latino fiction and nonfiction books. Examples of books included in the list are *Ole Flamenco, Rene Has Two Last Names,* and *De Colores.*

We also recommend that classrooms and school libraries increase the number of books in students' native languages. A recommended list of native language books (by grade level) should also be sent to parents so that they can take their children to the community library or purchase the books.

Although there are several strategies to get students motivated and engaged with literature texts, we recommend two strategies that traditionally have been successful in eliciting reading comprehension and writing development: literature response and dramatizations.

Literature Response

After reading a piece of literature in the native language, a group of students meets for a discussion. Each student expresses ideas, opinions, and reactions about the piece of literature read. Teachers guide students to a deeper understanding by asking them to support their points of view with information from the text (e.g., the setting, the main characters, the plot).

Dramatizations

This is a follow-up activity after reading and discussing a piece of literature, which provides students with an activity for stimulating creative imagination and opportunities for a deeper understanding of the text. The creative dramatization may take the mode of a role-play, improvised story, pantomime, or skit. Using the native language of the students is an asset in helping students to represent literature in the classroom.

HELPING STUDENTS BECOME INDEPENDENT WRITERS

Learning to write is developmentally important for nurturing literate individuals. Writing is a tool for self-expression, and it helps students organize and communicate their thinking. Writing in students' primary language provides them with opportunities to expand their cognitive/conceptual knowledge as well as provide a forum to express their creativity using a variety of writing modes (Calkins, 1994; Carrasquillo, Kucer, & Abrams, 2004; Peregoy & Boyle, 2005). Writing is also a manifestation of students' language and literacy understanding and their communication of meaning. Since students have developed a conceptual map in their primary language, and demonstrate mastery of listening and speaking skills and processes, as well as a reading foundation, writing comes easily as intertwined learning. The psychomotor act of writing enhances students' ability to read. The complementary relationship between reading and writing continues long after the early efforts. Writing in school must follow a rich language environment in which students are constantly involved in using writing to learn, to express meaning, and to communicate their own thinking. As shown in Figure 3.7, planning for the development of writing in students' primary language gives emphasis to the following three areas: topic, purpose, and audience.

The school curriculum requires students to become proficient writers in a variety of writing modes (narrative, descriptive, expository, persuasive), as well as with a diversity of topics and levels. In each of these modes, students are required to demonstrate grade-level writing proficiency. This writing proficiency is demonstrated when students write content that achieves the following: (1) focuses on a specific topic; (2) follows an organizational pattern containing a beginning, a middle, and an end, and uses transitional devices; (3) contains supporting ideas developed through the use of details or examples; and (4) follows the conventions of a given language with respect to punctuation, sentence structure, and spelling.

Educators can build students' writing through many writing initiatives; one of them is the use of regular writing prompts. The regular use of prompts provides students with practice building writing skills. The main aim of writing prompts is to give suggestions to the student to write on a diversity of topics. Prompts help students to think in a systematic way and come up with interesting pieces of writing. These prompts provide students with a diversity of writing emphases in order to convey/describe experiences, summarize information, and persuade others to accept a particular issue or opinion. These activities lead bilingual students to develop growth as writers in both their native language and English. Teachers support student writing using a variety of methods, such as writing prompts, teacher-student conferences, and class discussions. Parents who also encourage their children to write will contribute to their academic growth.

Figure 3.7. School Writing

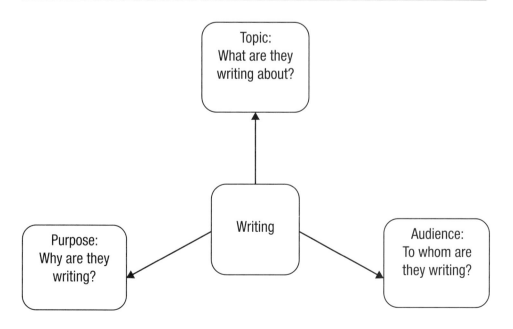

4

The Role of the Native Language in the English as a Second Language Classroom

Dear Teacher,

I would like to introduce you to my son, Wind-Wolf. He is probably what you would consider a typical Indian kid. He was born and raised on a reservation. He has black hair, dark brown eyes, and olive complexion. And like so many Indian children his age, he is shy and quiet in the classroom. He is 5 years old, in kindergarten, and I can't understand why you have already labeled him a "slow learner."

At the age of 5, he has already been through quite an education compared with his peers in Western society. At his first introduction into this world, he was bonded to his mother and to the Mother Earth in a traditional native childbirth ceremony. And he has been continuously cared for by his mother, father, sisters, cousins, uncles, grandparents, and extended tribal family since this ceremony.

So, dear teacher, I want to introduce you to my son, Wind-Wolf, who is not really a "typical" little Indian kid after all. He stems from a long line of hereditary chiefs, medicine men and women, and ceremonial leaders whose accomplishments and unique forms of knowledge are still being studied and recorded in contemporary books. He has seven different tribal systems flowing through his blood; he is even part white. I want my child to succeed in school and in life. I don't want him to be a dropout or juvenile delinquent or to end up on drugs and alcohol because he is made to feel inferior or because of discrimination. I want him to be proud of his rich heritage and culture, and I would like him to develop the necessary capabilities to adapt to, and succeed in, both cultures. But I need your help.

What you say and what you do in the classroom, what you teach and how you teach it, and what you don't say and don't teach will have a significant effect on the potential success or failure of my child. Please remember that this is the primary year of his education and development. All I ask is that you work with me, not against me, to help educate my child in the best way. If you don't have the knowledge, preparation, experience, or training to effectively deal with culturally different children, I am willing to help you with the few resources I have available or direct you to such resources. My Indian child has a constitutional right to learn, retain, and maintain his heritage and culture. By the same token, I strongly believe that non-Indian children also have a constitutional right to learn about our Native American heritage and culture, because Indians play a significant part in the history of Western society. Until this reality is equally understood and applied in education as a whole, there will be a lot more schoolchildren in grades K–2 identified as "slow learners."

> My son, Wind-Wolf, is not an empty glass coming into your class to be filled. He is a full basket coming into a different environment and society with something special to share. Please let him share his knowledge, heritage, and culture with you and his peers.
>
> (Robert Lake, a member of the Seneca and Cherokee Indian tribes, "An Indian Father's Plea")

English language learners in the United States participate in diverse instructional programs, including bilingual education, English as a Second Language, and English-only instruction. All of those programs require providing some type of assistance with English language development for students who have a primary language other than English (Carrasquillo, 1994). Usually, this language assistance is provided through a specialized approach called English as a Second Language, which is sensitive to students' needs, experiences, native languages, and cultural backgrounds. The content of this chapter addresses the role that native language plays in the English as a Second Language (ESL) classroom. This chapter attempts to answer the following questions: (1) What role does the native language play in the ESL classroom?; (2) What instructional factors contribute to effective instruction in second language classrooms?; (3) How does a teacher use the native language as a resource in the ESL classroom to enhance English language development?; (4) What methods and strategies are available to ESL educators, especially teachers, for providing effective instruction using the native language?; (5) What research-based instructional activities can teachers use to support native language and English language development?; and (6) What are the common practices of practitioners who are making use of the native language in their teaching?

ENGLISH AS A SECOND LANGUAGE PROGRAMS

In the United States, English as a Second Language (ESL) is the term used to describe an integral program for teaching a group of learners who are acquiring a second language, English in this case. An ESL program is the main approach used in U.S. school systems to address the need of second language learners to acquire English language skills (speaking, listening, reading, and writing) while learning academic content of the various subject areas. It is an instructional approach that focuses on a step-by-step methodology to develop English language skills (Hernandez-Sheets, 2005) for the purpose of acquiring academic learning. It can probably be said that ESL is a bridge from the development of language to academic subject matter in the English-only classroom. The main goal of ESL programs is to prepare students to function successfully in classrooms where English is the language of instruction. The objectives of an ESL program are systematic development in the following areas:

- Acquisition of a vocabulary for expressing oneself in different social and academic environments;
- Automatic control and fluency in the use of natural and accurate English language, linguistic, and grammatical patterns;
- Natural communication for meaningful interactions;
- Creation of grammatical and syntactical construction abilities;
- Development of strategies to confront the reading process and to attain varied skills of reading; and
- Development of conceptual, grammatical, and syntactical forms of writing.

ESL instruction enhances and develops students' linguistic and cognitive skills as well as content area knowledge. An ESL program includes the following characteristics: (1) emphasis on communication and meaning; (2) integration of the four areas of language for functional contexts of learning and communication development; (3) incorporation of students' prior linguistic, conceptual, and cultural experiences; (4) incorporation of content that includes traditions of students' cultural heritage; and (5) provision for the continuation of conceptual and linguistic development in the various content areas of the curriculum. Accordingly, an ESL classroom is one in which abstract concepts are simplified, vocabulary is monitored, and key words are used in conjunction with visuals in order for English learners to acquire the necessary academic and linguistic skills.

Free-Standing ESL: This type of program is not integrated with other school programs; it stands alone to meet the immediate communication and academic needs of English learners. This program may suit a school district with many languages or ethnic groups represented in the school and not too many students from one particular language group. Usually, language arts and the content areas are taught using second language instructional strategies.

Pull-out ESL: This type of program provides limited daily English language assistance in segregated classrooms. The teacher usually goes from classroom to classroom to teach a group of students from different grades identified as having the same level of English language proficiency.

Pull-in ESL: This type of program is language assistance offered to ELL students in their own classroom and based on the grade-level curriculum under study. The teacher usually goes to the classroom to work with the mainstream teacher using the same curriculum content with structured second language instructional strategies.

ESL in Bilingual Education: This is a structured English language assistance program designed for students enrolled in bilingual programs who are in the process of becoming bilingual and bicultural. It is usually taught in the bilingual classroom by the bilingual teacher or an assigned ESL teacher. The curriculum is usually based on the classroom grade level, modified to meet the linguistic needs of the students.

All ESL programs make use of effective second language instructional strategies to develop fluency in listening, speaking, reading, and writing English. The ESL classroom contains a variety of materials and resources, including bilingual dictionaries, technological devices that can translate from the student's native language to the second language and from the second language to the native language, and recording devices to enable teachers to record their students' voices. Teachers may use read-aloud strategies and emphasize development of academic vocabulary. The ESL program is key to the success of students' acquisition of English. Authorities in the field, including Diaz-Rico (2008); Echevarria, Vogt, & Short (2008); Herrera (2010); and Lessow-Hurley (2005), agree that ESL instruction is the most important tool for the development of English skills but they also agree that in many cases, the lack of acceptance of students' native language results in not using the native language as a resource in the ESL classroom.

BENEFITS OF USING THE NATIVE LANGUAGE IN THE ENGLISH AS A SECOND LANGUAGE CLASSROOM

Many benefits accrue to students who continue using their native language while learning a second language and receiving much of their instruction in the second language (in this case, English). Benefits include (1) self-regulation; (2) reading preparedness; (3) increased achievement; (4) increased opportunities for entertainment and enjoyment; and (5) increased opportunities for employment (Demmert & Towner, 2003). The cognitive capacity needed to switch between two languages improves a student's ability to focus on an individual task, and it also improves the ability for them to control themselves (Bialystok & Craik, 2010). For example, Carlson and Meltzoff (2008) found that increased self-regulation or "executive functioning" provides bilingual children with a significant benefit when it comes to "tasks that appear to call for managing conflicting attentional demands" (p. 295).

Herrera (2010) proposed that reading preparedness starts first and foremost with the language used at home. Reading preparedness includes phonemic awareness, phonics, vocabulary development, comprehension, and fluency. After the home environment, reading preparedness is influenced by sociocultural factors in the community as well as motivation of the learner. All students are cognitively, linguistically, and emotionally connected to the language of their home (Hernandez-Sheets, 2005). If more school personnel understood the process of second language acquisition and the importance that native language plays in success, academic achievement of bilingual students would increase. Bilingual learners make great strides and benefit immensely when educators value, build, and promote each student's dual-language knowledge and language continuity.

Teachers promote learning through positive attitudes and acts, including these: (1) valuing and using the linguistic knowledge students bring to school; (2) including instructional strategies to promote language development; (3) building linguistic continuity between the home and school to support student's social and cognitive development; and (4) recognizing that these linguistic strengths have been achieved through their first language (Hernandez-Sheets, 2005). Those strengths create instructional opportunities for ESL teachers and learning opportunities for bilingual students.

Use of the native language in teaching is of paramount importance because it is the foundation for students' understanding, and necessary in the provision of culturally competent instruction in bilingual settings. Teachers must acquire understanding of the linguistic abilities, similarities, and processes of using first and second language for academic success. Fortunately, "understanding how we acquire a second language is an exciting challenge because it engages all aspects of human nature." (Bialystok & Hakuta, 1994, p. 6). ESL teachers should allow, appreciate, and take delight when English learners use their native language and other prior knowledge as a bridge to language development in English.

In ESL classrooms, each student's native language is the catalyst for accelerating the academic success of each individual. Teachers must utilize the native language students bring into the classroom because it is crucial for making meaning of new concepts. Research indicates that second language learners may attain linguistic milestones in verbal, cognitive, and emotional communication in both languages (Genesee, 1989; Kovelman, Baker, & Petitto, 2008; Kovelman & Petitto, 2003) because human brains have dedicated areas for multiple language processing (Bialystok & Hakuta, 1994). Cardenas (1986) goes one step further and proposes the use of learners' native language in academic instruction for growth of self-concept. Moll, Amanti, Neff, & Gonzalez (1992) stated that children bring funds of knowledge to the classroom, and those funds of knowledge include the native language. Making connections between the native language and the second language is sensible when teaching ELLs, just as connecting prior knowledge to new knowledge makes sense. Herrera (2010) describes "linking language learning" as a strategy that becomes a source of connection throughout content teaching. When linking language learning, the teacher uses the native language of the student by signaling the importance and utility of the language, maximizing instruction, and ensuring conceptual comprehension. Authorities in the field of ESL, particularly August, Carlo, Dressler, and Snow (2005), have discussed the importance of native language in the instructional process. They consider the native language to be an important resource for comprehension and connecting second language vocabulary to academic achievement in the content areas. The primary language of the students, along with its traditions and background, must become an important component of the curriculum and of the instruction.

THE NATIVE LANGUAGE AS AN INSTRUCTIONAL SUPPORT

There are reasons supporting the use of the native language in the second language classroom.

1. Knowledge learned through one language paves the way for knowledge acquisition in the second language. Research shows that practices incorporating bilingual students' native languages into instruction is a major factor in enhancing their success in school (Bialystok & Hakuta, 1994; Karathanos, 2009; Lessow-Hurley, 2005). Bilingual learners instructed in their first language attained or surpassed the achievement levels of their peers who were educated in English-only classrooms (Bialystok & Hakuta, 1994; Lessow-Hurley, 2005). Second language learners transfer concepts and principles already learned in their first language into the second language. Having instruction available to the students in their native language allows them to comprehend instruction, which enables them to achieve success in the mainstream classroom.

2. Use of native language validates learners' home language and culture. Nieto (2000) emphasizes the need to affirm diversity and to recognize the strengths that students bring into the classroom. Educators who affirm diversity embrace students' identities, which are formed in part by the connections to their native language. By drawing on their cultural backgrounds, educators work toward the development of desirable bilingual students' states of mind as identified in Figure 4.1.

Bilingual students themselves are a great asset in ESL classrooms and in content area classrooms because the students can share their knowledge, language, and traditions, which enhances the knowledge of others. Such sharing may even increase English language ability in native English speakers (e.g., Spanish and English share many Latin root words); provide new perspectives on historical issues; and increase cultural appreciation. Bilingual students and their families have many assets to share with a school and community.

Denying the use of the native language makes students feel as if their language is not valid or unimportant, which by extension invalidates their culture, family, and personal identity. A society able to celebrate and cherish the heritage of diverse cultures is mutually beneficial to all citizens. Educators who are aware of these students' language, culture, and experiences will provide instructional support to ELLs. An educator who understands language diversity recognizes the native language as an opportunity to help a student use two languages effectively. An educator who respects the language and the culture of all learners honors those students and provides for them an opportunity to excel cognitively, linguistically, academically, and socially.

Figure 4.1. Desirable States of Mind for Bilingual Students

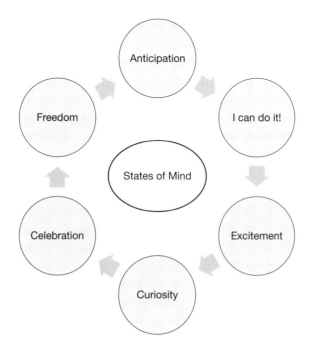

3. School and instructional activities that embrace students' native language, culture, and background encourage higher levels of parental involvement in children's learning. Parents want a better future for their children, and educators are well advised to work in collaboration with parents. Often, bilingual students become translators, enabling communication regarding educational transactions between parents and educators. Many bilingual students and their families need to feel welcomed and accepted in their school and community. Families are partners in the education of ELLs and critical to the vitality of schools. When educators deny the opportunity to convey a message in the native language, bilingual students and their families may lose trust in the teachers and the administrators. Once educators earn the trust of the family, in return, they will share all of their resources and will be able to establish pedagogical relationships between the teacher and family, which will also contribute to relationships between the school and the community.

4. The native language can be used to bridge instruction. The students' native language can be used as a bridge to the second language, enabling students to ask, to inform, to clarify, and to summarize information, for instance. We have heard many bilingual learners say that school personnel have penalized them for speaking their native language in school (Rodríguez, Ringler, O'Neal, & Bunn 2009). On the contrary, educators should make use of the native language to bridge instruction. For example, the use of cognates is highly recommended for conceptual and linguistic understanding (Herrera, 2010). Figure 4.2 describes vocabulary word transfers (cognates) from Spanish to English in three subject areas. These cognates are bridge strategies that increase vocabulary. Calderón (2007) and Herrera (2010) reinforce the idea that teachers need to teach vocabulary comprehension in order to accelerate academic comprehension. An educator who provides bridges from native language to second language enhances academic comprehension and the likelihood of success for ELLs. We recommend that educators emphasize the need to promote cross-language transfer of knowledge (linguistic and academic) from native language to second language.

Figure 4.2. Cognates in English, History, and Mathematics

English	History	Mathematics
analogía/analogy	agricultura/agriculture	área/area
biografía/biography	cronología/chronology	base/base
debate/debate	colonia/colony	círculo/circle
definición/definition	expedición/expedition	convertir/convert
editar/edit	hemisferio/hemisphere	decimal/decimal
novela/novel	idea/idea	distancia/distance
contraste/contrast	justicia/justice	división/division
propósito/purpose	sociedad/society	geométrico/geometric

Source: Herrera, 2010, p. 96.

5. Second language learners who learned to read in their native language demonstrated enhanced phonological awareness and English reading skills. Phonological awareness has been shown to be a good predictor of later reading ability (Cummins, 1984, 2000; Freeman & Freeman, 2004). Carreira (2007) advocates for schools to use culture and language in teaching as a way to draw on knowledge in order to increase each child's awareness of and ability to manipulate sounds, which is the basic foundation for reading preparedness. A study of bilingual children in Taiwan found that children who learned to read in their native language demonstrated enhanced phonological awareness and other reading skills (Fang-Ying, 2009). Brice and Roseberry-McKibbin (2001) explicitly stated that the native language adds to the child's ability to communicate in the second language.

Based on this extensive evidence, school districts, schools, and teachers are well advised to support English and native language biliteracy for bilingual students learning English. This may be done by using bilingual resources to enhance learning across the curriculum. Carreira goes further, arguing that school administrators should facilitate a cross-cultural model that socializes or accustoms bilingual students and parents to the American system of education. Valdés (1997) advised the pursuit of these four instructional goals: (1) native language maintenance; (2) acquisition of a prestige variety of native language styles and formats; (3) expansion of students' bilingual range (including grammatical, textual, and pragmatic competence); and (4) transfer of literacy skills from one language to the other.

In our own quest to identify strategies and approaches to bridge instruction using students' native language in the ESL classroom, we went into the field to observe successful ESL teachers. Such inquiry led us to develop the Native Language Instruction Foundation (NaLIF) Approach in order to provide a guide for teachers as they seek to instruct ELLs effectively through use of culture and first language.

THE NATIVE LANGUAGE INSTRUCTIONAL FOUNDATION (NaLIF) APPROACH

As we have stated repeatedly, each student's native language is an important cognitive asset for acquiring new knowledge, skills, and capabilities. This has been emphasized by many authorities, including Thomas and Collier (1997, 2002) and Valdés (1997), who stated that in order to provide effective educational opportunities for bilingual students, educators have to deliver academic instruction that fosters and facilitates academic and cognitive growth in two languages. The Native Language Instructional Foundation (NaLIF) Approach is an instructional problem-solving strategy that uses the native language and the second language flexibly to create and adapt instruction that will improve the academic, cognitive, and social achievements of students. As shown in Figure 4.3, NaLIF gives teachers a guide for the design, development, and delivery of effective instruction in the second language classroom. The cognitive strategies involved in using two languages posit that the instructional tasks tap into the bilingual functioning of the brain. NaLIF helps teachers to move students' cognitive and language development to the next level of proficiency. We briefly describe the steps in NaLIF.

Figure 4.3. Components of the Native Language Instructional Foundation (NaLIF) Approach

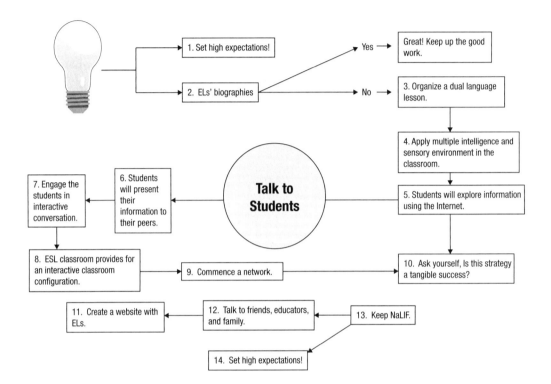

Step 1: Set high expectations! When teachers believe that students are capable of excelling at high academic levels and that they will be capable of attending colleges and universities, the teachers set high expectations and provide a learning environment conducive to intellectual and social growth.

Step 2: NaLIF guides educators to learn their students' biographies in order to anchor their teaching. As discussed by Herrera (2010), the use of culturally and linguistically driven biographies in instruction is instrumental in the education of bilingual students throughout the process of second language acquisition. Once educators understand the biographies of their bilingual students, teachers can develop effective instruction by utilizing, to the maximum extent, the student's native language to promote cognitive and sociocultural learning. Many teachers have used biography cards to learn about their students (see an example in Figure 4.4). NaLIF encourages teachers to be creative and to consider and use multiple instructional strategies.

Step 3: Plan dual-language lessons. This strategy includes the use of key terms and academic concepts in the students' native language and in the second language. This is the time to search the Internet for activities to help learners make connections between the two languages.

Figure 4.4. A Biography Card

Student Information	L1 Proficiency	L2 Proficiency
Name: Rosario Sánchez	**Oral:** Superior/Proficient	**Oral:** Intermediate
Age: 12	**Writing:** High Intermediate	**Writing:** Low Intermediate
Grade: 7th	**Reading:** Proficient	**Reading:** Low Intermediate
Born: USA	Based on tests and teacher classroom data. Scored high in the Spanish LAB-R.	Based on tests and teacher classroom data. Scored below average on the English LAB-R.
Time in USA: Ll–12 years	Demonstrates classroom academic work commensurate with L1 language proficiency	Demonstrates progress, especially in reading comprehension

Prior Schooling: All schooling in U.S. public schools

Parental Support: The student's family participates in school parental activities and attends individual meetings.

Academic/Assessment Considerations: The student likes to be involved in learning activities, but does not always follow class protocols. Student should be allowed to work in pairs on collaborative team projects, and to read in both languages at home and in school.

Source: Adapted from Herrera, 2010, p. 64. Used with permission.

Step 4: The use of multiple intelligence and sensory environment activities or tasks. These activities facilitate words as a link to academic language vocabulary. Gardner (1983, 2006) recognized linguistic, logical mathematics, musical, body kinesthetic, spatial, interpersonal, intrapersonal, existentialism, spirituality, and naturalism as multiple intelligences of learners. Figure 4.5 identifies instructional methods that are aligned with particular intelligences.

These activities become more interesting when the teacher incorporates them into instructional environments that include visuals, listening, touching, smelling, and tasting to enhance language learning and cognitive and social growth. These activities should be taught in the students' native language and in English in order to give students a sense of empowerment in the two languages.

Step 5: Ask the students to use the Internet to search for information, a fact, or a news item from their own language or culture. After students find the information, they may be asked to summarize it briefly in English. Students should be able to make the first and second language connection to process and deliver the information. By linking multiple intelligences with academic language vocabulary, students will be able to acquire the necessary skills and knowledge to become academically successful.

Step 6: Students present the information acquired to their peers. Students may choose the form of presentation, such as an oral presentation, a written narrative, a PowerPoint presentation, a drawing, or a cartoon.

Figure 4.5. Multiple Intelligences and Academic Language Vocabulary

Multiple Intelligences	Examples of Academic Language Vocabulary
Linguistics	Learn words in a foreign language; use diverse crosswords puzzles; find a word in the dictionary and put it in a sentence; choose specific words from a book and allow the students to relate the words to their own lives; explore prefixes and suffixes.
Logical Mathematics	Encode words; use math flash cards; connect numbers to form an image; use logic puzzles such as Sudoku; use number puzzles; use games such as Math Bingo and Jigsaw.
Music	Allow the students to make a song and to sing it in the classroom; mimic the sound of an instrument; put a rhythm to a word.
Body Kinesthetic	Mimic an animal; in a group, allow the students to form a machine or a word using their bodies; learn the deaf alphabet; clap each syllable of a word; change the arrangement of the classroom; go on field trips; find the meaning of a dance term and dance it.
Spatial	Draw words in different styles and colors; incorporate Pictionary; arrange words to form an object; take a photo of the meaning of a word; create a map of a story.
Interpersonal	With a partner, help each other determine the meaning of a word; use group work to play a game; play in group scrabbles; implement classroom parties; form discussion groups.
Intrapersonal	Have students set personal goals for class; allow students to make journal entries; allow students to edit their own writing and evaluate their own goals; identify challenges.
Existentialism	Have students compare traditional and contemporary morals and values considered in movies; have students create obituaries; have students define abstract concepts such as happiness.
Spirituality	Have students participate in yoga, meditate, paint, or engage in another form of artistic expression.
Naturalistic	Teach in the outdoors when identifying clouds or classifying plants and insects, studying the cosmos, or imitating sounds of bugs.

Step 7: Provide interactive conversations. Group students by languages, by interests, by countries, or by preferred subject area. Students will be provided with an outline to encourage conversations with other students in order to increase motivation, improve language skills, and to assess learning. Knowing students is necessary for creating multiple groups over the course of a semester or academic year. That is why the premise of NaLIF is to establish connections to students by getting to know them. Teachers need to ask themselves what they want their students to learn and how to make learning experiences meaningful to them. Learning language skills needs to have a purpose. Allow students time to have conversations in the language of their preference. Then ask one or two students to summarize what they learned.

Step 8: The ESL classroom provides for an interactive classroom configuration. We recommend including a variety of instructional experiences from total class group work, small-group work, work with one partner, and individual work.

Example 1: Using the content unit of social studies, students work in small groups to develop a project together. Example: In which state of the United States would you prefer to live? Why? Provide three facts and three ideas.

Example 2: Two students may search the Internet to resolve a question related to the science class. Example: If the sun is at the essentially same distance from Earth every day, how can there be parts of the planet in summer and other parts in winter?

Step 9: Start building a network. This network may include school agency partners, community organizers, parents, guardians, teachers, counselors, social workers, teacher assistants, siblings, and others who will assist a teacher with acquiring resource materials and providing instructional experiences that are meaningful to second language learners.

Step 10: At this point in NaLIF, it is time to consider whether the instructional strategy you selected has been a tangible success. How do you plan to evaluate the success of your students' learning? You need to collect data on how your students are attaining second language skills and making the connection with the native language. You also need to assess knowledge of subject matter and ability to apply knowledge in practice.

Step 11: Create a webpage with your students. The webpage may be related to the concepts learned, which connect academic language to the concepts.

Step 12: Talk to friends, educators, and family members. Recognize native language as a valuable asset that bilingual students bring into the classroom, and, most necessary, advocate for using native language in instruction.

Step 13: Continue using the NaLIF in a regular basis

Step 14: It is important to have a positive attitude about your student by setting high expectations.

Drawing on NaLIF helps to develop effective instruction through which learners may proceed through desirable states of mind during the learning process. The desirable states of mind motivate ELLs and enable them to make connections from their first language to the second language as they develop fluency in the second language. States of mind vary from day to day, hour to hour, and with digital communication, the potential for variation from minute to minute has increased. The point is that teachers need to work diligently and try different motivational and instructional tactics to connect with their students in order to help them learn. When educators appeal to the students' anticipation, efficacy (by nurturing in students an "I can do it!" attitude), excitement, and curiosity—success and ultimately freedom will follow.

NaLIF fosters bilingual education as well as ESL education with an emphasis on use of the native language for academic and sociocultural development. Using the NaLIF model, educators are encouraged to think of lesson planning in three phases: before, during, and after learner engagement, which encompasses the entire teaching cycle. This approach guides teachers to plan and deliver lessons in light of the bilingual students' biographies, including some level of native language development, promoting vocabulary instruction in both languages, and developing engaging literacy instruction.

COMPREHENSIBLE INPUT

Prior knowledge enables conceptual connections when the input is comprehensible. Learners connect comprehensible input (clarification, nonverbal feedback) to previously acquired linguistic competence and extra-linguistic knowledge, including contextual knowledge (Krashen, 1982). Attention to comprehensible input is necessary to acquire new knowledge of language structures. We offer the following recommendations to help teachers promote conceptual development through comprehensible input.

Recommendation 1: Integration of Language and Content. Bilingual learners face enormous challenges to learn content area information while acquiring a second language. The second language cannot be taught in a vacuum (i.e., separate from prior knowledge). Consequently, we recommend using concepts and content students already know in their first language to create a bridge to learning new language structures. Instruction that includes content from multiple subject areas helps to fill knowledge gaps.

Recommendation 2: Implementation of Grade-Level Curriculum. Educators need to ensure equity for all students, including bilingual learners, and to create learning opportunities in schools that will make possible the attainment of a high quality of life. The ESL curriculum must provide programmatic goals, objectives, and instructional strategies that match general curriculum standards and guidelines.

Recommendation 3: Cooperative Learning Activities. Second language learners can benefit from being paired with a partner or being placed in a small group. Approaches may include partnering with another student who speaks his or her native language to help scaffold and support learning. Alternatively, ELLs can be paired with English-speaking partners to help them adjust to the language and to learn. Importantly, bilingual students need to be able to work with supportive classmates to help maximize learning. When students interact with others, they construct meaning from new ideas and concepts while also sharing their unique background knowledge.

Recommendation 4: Integration of Cross-Cultural Reading Activities. One of the most effective ways to teach children to develop language skills, acquire content knowledge, and develop a love of reading is to *read to them*! By being read to daily, ELLs learn how to read with expression; they are able to match pictures with words; and they learn content knowledge as well. When reading to ELLs, teachers may accompany the readings with pictures, gestures, and dramatic voice in order to convey meaning. This is especially helpful for kindergarteners, 1st-, and 2nd-graders who are learning to read themselves. Students benefit when teachers and parents use cross-cultural literature, preferably in more than one language.

NATIVE LANGUAGE INSTRUCTION: PERSPECTIVES FROM THE FIELD

From ESL teachers we often hear the same message of this schoolteacher: "In my beginning professional years of teaching, I had many non-English-speaking students placed in my class. I often wondered why I was so fortunate to have these students under my tutelage. I can only say that these students were placed under my care for two reasons: one being that I was compassionate about their predicament. The second reason was I was the less combative teacher! If I knew then what I know now, I am convinced that I could really have helped them much of more of what I did with them to be academically successful."

(María E. Santiago, Florida)

This statement speaks to the indefatigable quest of teachers to do better and more when teaching English language learners. We take this opportunity to present the following reflections (of an ESL teacher, a parent, and a school principal) to convey different perspectives on the role of the native language in the ESL classroom. In each case, the reflection is prompted by a question.

An ESL Teacher Perspective

Question: How do I integrate students' native language and culture in my teaching?

I am an ESL teacher, teaching in an elementary school pull-out program. I pull out students with the same proficiency level from grades 1 and 2, and through small-group instruction or individualized instruction, I guide them to develop higher levels of literacy. I emphasize the native language and the cultural prior knowledge of my students by implementing a linking language learning approach.

(Ricardo Paredes, ESL teacher, North Carolina)

A Parent Perspective

Question: How did my child's teacher include our mother tongue and culture?

I am an immigrant parent from El Salvador. My two children and I have been in the United States for 2 years and they are presently enrolled in 7th and 10th grades. Although I do not speak or read English, I communicate in Spanish. The teacher who is helping my two kids with English is using some ways of teaching that make me feel that the instruction is like the one my two kids encountered in El Salvador. The teacher cares. She has taken the time to get to know my family and the community where we live. I think that she wants my children to succeed in the United States. I trust her; she told me that she has collected information about organizations that help parents like me understand the school system in the United States, and she has given me a list of those organizations.

(Silvia Rosario, Florida; translated from Spanish to English by the authors)

A School Principal Perspective

School principals are key players in the implementation of programs and curriculum initiatives in meeting the needs of a diverse student population. The following school principal's voice presents a positive attitude toward learning and teaching.

The curriculum that ESL teachers in my school implement is based on the new Common Core Learning Standards, which means that bilingual students are expected to learn the same content that all students are expected to master at their grade level. I guide my bilingual and ESL teachers to collaborate with mainstream teachers and show them strategies to use in providing comprehensible input especially using students' strongest language and culture. Teaching concepts and relating them to students' backgrounds is key to helping activate prior knowledge and linking that to new knowledge. Teachers use visuals, graphic organizers, and other instructional strategies that help provide multiple ways to process learning and also show learning.

(Rosita Rodríguez, school principal, New York)

Educators must be prepared to offer bilingual students a high-quality curriculum and instructional experience, rich with English language learning strategies that make use of the native language as a resource. Qualified and well-trained ESL teachers greatly contribute to that conceptualization.

5

Native Language Instruction
in Dual-Language Programs

A school, two bridges and a skyline
with parents all over the building
building bi-lingual bridges
through language classes,
in Haitian-Creole, Korean, Spanish and Chinese
with common core curriculum standards
presented to students in different languages
totally nurtured within a cross-cultural content.

(Angela Carrasquillo, "Bi-lingual Bridges")

This chapter addresses dual language in the United States from the perspective of language minority students who speak a primary language other than English, and who are learning English in school. These students are learning in their native language (e.g., Spanish, Mandarin, Korean, Navajo) as one of the two languages used for instruction in dual-language programs. After the reauthorization of the Elementary and Secondary Education Act (ESEA) in 1994, the United States Department of Education promoted education programs whose goal was dual-language competency for two types of public school students: language minority students with limited or no proficiency in English, and those whose home language was solely English. These programs were designed to create dual-language competencies in students without sacrificing their success in school. And due to this federal effort, bilingual dual-language programs in the United States have increased. State education departments followed the federal initiative, providing funding for dual/two-way bilingual programs. Given the fact that students who were instructed in these federal and state-funded programs performed academically well, local school districts began promoting and funding instruction in two languages. However, in spite of the increase of bilingual dual-language programs, and the abundance of published literature on their academic benefits, there is not enough information on how to promote the native language component of language minority/bilingual students.

This chapter provides a general overview on dual-language development and implementation, with emphasis given to the area of native language curriculum and instruction. It includes a brief overview of the goals and objectives of dual-language instruction, a brief research-based rationale on its effectiveness, as well as various teaching, learning, and assessment strategies, in addition to activities that promote native language literacy.

The chapter attempts to answer the following questions: (1) What are the main theoretical and research principles guiding the implementation of dual-language programs?; (2) What does current research say about a quest for making students biliterate and bilingual?; (3) Which instructional strategies and practices facilitate the acquisition of literacy in students' first language?; and (4) What classroom assessment tools are useful in measuring bilingual students' biliteracy growth? The focus of the chapter is on describing dual-language programs for bilingual students, especially those whose primary language is a language other than English.

GUIDING PRINCIPLES FOR DUAL-LANGUAGE INSTRUCTION

Dual-language teaching is a developmental, language-enriched, instructional program in which instruction is provided in two languages as the medium of communication and learning. Students learn curriculum content, literacy, as well as a new language (Christian, 2011; Lessow-Hurley, 2005; Lindholm & Aclan, 1991; Lindholm-Leary, 2004/2005; Lyster, 2007). There is a rich literature (Calderón & Minaya-Rowe, 2003; Carrasquillo & Buttaro, 2006; Cloud, Genesee, & Hamayan, 2000; Freeman & Freeman, 2004; Freeman, Freeman, & Mercuri, 2005; Lessow-Hurley, 2005; Soltero, 2004) that clearly presents information on the different types of program approaches, models, and organizational structures. Evidence suggests that dual-language programs have the potential to foster significant academic achievement; bilingualism and biliteracy; development of higher-order thinking skills; and increased cultural awareness and understanding in the students served (Christian, 2011; Hough, 2009; Thomas & Collier, 2002, 2003a).

In the United States, the goal of most dual-language programs is to provide high-quality instruction for students who start school primarily speaking a language other than English, and simultaneously, to provide instruction in a second language for English proficient students. The rationale for students who are learning English as a Second Language is that English skills are best acquired by students who have strong oral and literacy skills in their native language (Cummins, 1981; Lyster, 2007). It has been hypothesized that a great majority of students who participate in dual-language instruction for three or more years (1) meet or exceed federal, state, and district/school learning standards; (2) achieve grade-level literacy in the first and second languages; (3) develop positive cross-cultural attitudes, behaviors, and skills that will help them function in a global society; and (4) demonstrate high levels of self-esteem (Thomas & Collier, 2002, 2003b; Sugerman & Howard, 2001).

The rationale for native English speakers who participate in dual-language instruction is that these students can acquire advanced second language skills (e.g., Spanish, Polish, Korean) without compromising their first language development or academic achievement. The native language of the students is nurtured, moving these students toward bilingualism and biliteracy. This instructional approach allows students to achieve balanced language proficiency by providing high levels of content knowledge accessible in two languages, and by developing metacognitive and cognitive strategies to learn grade-level school curriculum. The rationale behind the integration of native English speakers and native speakers of other languages is that the interaction of the two languages facilitates second language acquisition, promoting natural and substantive interaction among speakers of different languages.

Not all bilingual dual-language programs are the same. They vary in name, student population, language allocation, and language emphasized throughout the content areas. For example, the following names are currently used to identify this programmatic instructional approach.

- Two-Way Bilingual
- Two-Way Immersion
- Dual-Language Immersion
- Dual-Language Program

Dual-language classrooms may be linguistically homogeneous or may include speakers of both languages for instruction. Although there are many variations in the student population, it is common to find the following language groups within dual-language programs.

Group 1: Dual-language program for *monolingual* English speakers: Monolingual English speakers learning through two languages, the native language (English), and a second language.

- L1: English
- L2: Spanish, Chinese, Korean, or any other language

Group 2: Dual-language program for bilingual students. It includes students who are not proficient or completely proficient in English.

Program A
- L1: Spanish, Mandarin, Korean, or any other language
- L2: English

Program B
- L1: English dominant but not proficient
- L2: Spanish, Chinese, Korean, or any other language

Some children are exposed to their parents' native language and English from birth; others are only exposed to their parents' native language (or home language) from birth and are not exposed to English until later. There is another group of students who were born outside the United States who bring a strong home language foundation and no English exposure at all.

There are also variations in the language allocation for instruction. Among the most popular,

50/50: Equal language allocation
90/10: L1/L2
80/20: L1/L2

There are subject area language emphases depending on school philosophy and goals. For example, the subject of mathematics may be taught using one of the following language modes:

- Math taught in L1 only
- Math: Day 1, taught in L1; Day 2, taught in L2
- Math: Week 1, taught in L1; Week 2, taught in L2

Dual-language classrooms typically divide their days or weeks between the two languages of instruction, expecting all class members to interact in only one language at a time. Current implementation prefers a 50/50 model in which students are exposed to the two languages in all the content areas as well as language arts. Teachers teach both languages through content, according to program design decisions. For example, mathematics is taught in Spanish by Teacher A one day of the week, followed by mathematics taught in English the next day by Teacher B. Teacher B continues the mathematics lesson in English that was initiated in Spanish by Teacher A the day before. Another implementation may have Teacher A providing all instruction in L1 while Teacher B teaches all subjects in L2. Another approach is to assign Teacher A to teach mathematics or science in L1 with Teacher B teaching social studies in L2. Students learn content in both languages, and teachers adapt instruction to ensure students' conceptual development and comprehension through meaningful lessons, vocabulary building, and acquisition of oral and written language structures, which promote bilingualism and biliteracy (Center for Applied Linguistics, 2012; Parkes & Ruth, 2009).

Within each language group, bilingual students vary greatly in their ability to understand and communicate in the two languages. One primary reason is the timing and emphasis the school places on students' exposure to English instruction, the majority language in most schools and the language for the majority of students' assessment of learning and academic growth.

The majority of dual-language programs are implemented at the elementary school level, but there are some at the secondary (middle and high school) level (Center for Applied Linguistics, 2012). Secondary school students are at a stage where fitting in and asserting independence often pushes them away from dual-language programs that may be seen as a continuation of elementary school, a separation from peers, or a limitation on opportunities to participate in electives such as athletics, fine arts, or technology. However, recently more secondary dual-language programs are being implemented due to the public's acceptance of these programs, and more parents being interested in their children becoming bilingual and biliterate. Most English dual-language programs in the United States operate in English and Spanish for demographics reasons but others pair English with Cantonese, French, Korean, Mandarin, Japanese, and Navajo at the elementary level.

Dual-language programs must identify clear outcomes for students and parents. For example, the goals of a dual-language program at the high school level may include "prepare students with 21st-century skills so that they may compete in a global society," since proficiency in more than one language is critical to local and global competitiveness. Another goal of the program may emphasize pursuit of a college career that requires professionals to be bilingual to better serve clients. Then, the focus of the dual-language program would be the provision of college career standards in both languages (e.g., English and the target language). Guided by goals that convey high expectations, instruction in two languages enables dual-language students to develop confidence, depth and breadth of vocabulary across all content areas, and the mental ability to perform in the two languages.

Regardless of grade level, all dual-language program planners, participants, teachers, and supporters need to determine what they want dual-language students to be able to do with the native and target language, in what contexts, and with what level of proficiency—and then plan for its implementation and success. If the goal is equal or on-grade-level performance in both languages across content areas, then the students' opportunities to wrestle cognitively with the program languages must be varied, have depth and complexity, and develop appropriate structures for the discipline, the language, and the audience.

BENEFITS OF DUAL-LANGUAGE PROGRAMS

Dual-language programs are supported by research that demonstrates the cognitive and academic benefits of learning in two languages, and becoming bilingual and biliterate. A brief summary of research identifying successful results of dual-language programs follows.

High Levels of Academic Achievement

There is substantial evidence to support dual-language education as a viable and enriching method of supporting high levels of academic achievement (Christian, 2011; Lyster, 2007; Estrada, Gómez, & Ruiz-Escalante, 2009; Thomas & Collier, 2002, 2003b). Studies report higher levels of academic achievement for students who participate in dual-language programs versus those enrolled in other bilingual or mainstream English classrooms (Alanis & Rodriguez, 2008; Christian, 1994, 2011; Collier & Thomas, 2004; Smith & Arnot-Hopffer, 1998; Sugerman & Howard, 2001; Thomas & Collier, 2002, 2003a). The Thomas and Collier studies (2002, 2003a, 2003b) followed dual-language programs in districts of varying size in 15 states for nearly 20 years and concluded that dual-language instruction is a unique program that facilitates high levels of academic achievement in students.

For example, Thomas and Collier (2002) analyzed achievement data of a group of students from Houston, and they reported that English language learners/emergent bilinguals who received 5 years of dual-language schooling reached the 51st percentile on the Stanford 9—a nationally normed test in English—after having initially qualified 5 years earlier for English language services by scoring low on English proficiency tests.

Christian (1994) compared students enrolled in a dual-language program to a control population, and found that 3rd-graders from the Amigos dual-immersion programs in Cambridge, Massachusetts, outperformed Spanish-speaking students who were enrolled in another type of bilingual education program in reading and mathematics when tested in both Spanish and English, and performed at grade-level norm for children their age, which included English-only speaking students. The Center for

Applied Linguistics (2012) collected data on the language development and academic achievement of students in Spanish/English dual-language programs across the country and they found that both native English speakers and native Spanish speakers showed progress in their language and literacy skills.

Bilingual Proficiency and Biliteracy

Bilingual students who enroll in dual-language programs develop both oral proficiency *and* literacy in two languages (Carrasquillo, 2011; Collier & Thomas, 1989, 2004; Ray, 2009; Smith & Arnot-Hopffer, 1998), simultaneously or successively, due to the supporting effect of one language on the other one. A key variable in determining the cognitive benefits associated with bilingualism is the achievement of a balanced state of bilingualism and biliteracy. Research conducted by Kirk Senesac (2002), Lindholm and Aclan (1991), and Lindholm-Leary (2004/2005) indicates that students in dual-language programs are able to achieve this balanced state, as dual-language programs use specially tailored curriculum and instruction that fosters equally high levels of content knowledge in two languages (Ray, 2009). Christian (1994) showed information of Spanish-dominant children at the Key School, in Arlington, Virginia, in which Spanish-dominant students demonstrated oral English fluency by 3rd grade. English writing samples collected from native Spanish speakers in 5th and 6th grades were indistinguishable from those of native English speakers, and all were of high quality. García (2005) found that the writing development of participating dual-language students (English/Spanish, and English/Chinese) in San Francisco reached grade-level benchmarks by the 3rd-grade level.

But the literature also points out that these positive results are not immediate, as progress is not typically seen until at least 3 years after dual-language instruction begins (Alanis & Rodríguez, 2008; Bialystok, Luk & Kwan, 2005; Cobb, Vega, & Kronauge, 2009). A dual-language program with a duration of less than 3 years of implementation is insufficient and will not show high achievement levels, bilingualism, or biliteracy. Therefore, it must have a minimum duration of 3 years of implementation, with the recommendation of extending it as long as possible through the later grades. The longer students remain in a well-developed and implemented program, the better and deeper the development of language and literacy skills the students will demonstrate.

Development of Cross-Cultural Awareness

Effective dual-language instruction depends on the implementation of a bilingual environment at the school level, which supports the development of language and enhances both groups of students' self-esteem and cross-cultural understanding (Alanis & Rodríguez, 2008; Christian, 1994; Collier & Thomas, 2004; Estrada, Gómez, & Ruiz-Escalante, 2009). When looking at teachers' self-efficacy in a bilingual/dual-language program, Ray (2009) noted that in the United States, the dual-language model for English learners is additive in nature, seeking to add English to the student's body of knowledge while at the same time maintaining the first language. Parchia (2000) conducted a study on African American parents and children who were participating in dual-language schools, and found that these schools did a far superior job at offering students integrated cross-cultural experiences than the monolingual schools with which they had contact. In addition, parents and children who were interviewed expressed that although their own particular cultural or academic concerns were not directly reflected in the programs in which they were enrolled (the programs focused more on Latino culture), they chose to stay in these programs to enhance future educational and job successes through the acquisition of an additional language and cross-cultural skills.

According to Freeman, Freeman, and Mercuri (2005), dual-language programs have raised the status and importance of languages other than English in many communities across the United States. These programs have helped build cross-cultural school communities and cross-cultural friendships among students and parents, relationships that probably would not have developed without the programs. They also argue that dual-language programs raise the status of languages other than English, because as native English-speaking children become bilingual, parents and students alike see the value of knowing more than one language. In addition, as community leaders, school board members, school administrators, and teachers work together to design and implement dual-language programs, this cooperation enriches all parties and their perceptions of polylingualism.

IMPLEMENTATION INDICATORS

Positive outcomes of dual-language programs require a long-term commitment from administrators, teachers, and parents (Cloud, Genesee, & Hamayan, 2000; Mora, Wink & Wink, 2001). Their commitment results in successful programs that reflect the following seven components.

Administration's Commitment to Bilingualism, Biliteracy, and Bilingual Education

Dual-language instruction has the greatest impact when the entire school's staff believes in bilingualism plus promotes and encourages the implementation of bilingual programming. Gomez, Freeman, and Freeman (2005) state that effective programs must be implemented systematically and provided with adequate administrative, faculty, and resource support. If not well implemented, critics of bilingual education will use the data from poorly conceived or implemented programs to campaign against bilingual education in general. And worse, students will not receive the true benefits of a sound dual-language program.

Equal Status of Both Languages

Both languages are seen as important learning and instructional vehicles in the development of knowledge, concepts and academic language. Scheduling is such that instruction in both languages shares the same level of importance and amount of time for the development of language and content. In addition, the school promotes a bilingual environment in which general announcements, written communication, displays, and other communicative tools are done in the two languages.

Challenging Grade-Level Curriculum

It is well established that the challenging task of attaining academic proficiency in two languages requires a high level of abstract cognitive processing (Hadi-Tabassum, 2005), increased cognitive skills, and consistent meaningful exposure to the content areas (Stewart, 2005). In well-implemented dual-language programs, the curriculum contains clear instructional objectives in language arts and the content areas, enriched by themes related to students' backgrounds and cultures, and students engage in learning while not showing any concern for the "identified language of the day." For them, it is a natural process that on "Monday, all the instruction is in English and then, the next day (Tuesday) teaching and learning is provided in Haitian-Creole." It is common to see students at the beginning of the dual-language learning experience demonstrating some level of language ambivalence, an initial tendency to only use the strongest language in their personal communication with peers. This behavior is mainly seen in the first 2 years of dual-language implementation (e.g., kindergarten and 1st grade) and less frequently in the following years.

Teacher Effectiveness in Delivering Instruction

Research has consistently documented that the best way to improve the education of students is to provide them with qualified and effective teachers as well as effective classroom instruction (August & Shanahan, 2006; Carrasquillo & Rodríguez, 2002; Genesee, Lindholm-Leary, Saunders, & Christian, 2006; Slavin & Calderón, 2001). Complete understanding of the goals and philosophy of the bilingual program is crucial for teachers (Cloud, Genesee, & Hamayan, 2000). Carrasquillo (2011) observed a group of dual-language teachers for 3 months in a dual-language school in New York City in order to identify type and frequency of research-based instructional strategies used in the promotion of language and literacy. She found that the teachers who had a strong understanding of dual-language instruction, especially its philosophy and goals, were very successful in creating an instructional setting in which students were willing to take risks with both languages, and they demonstrated engagement in learning. Those observed teachers made instructional decisions based on the needs of their students, and implemented a variety of teaching practices, which ultimately resulted in students' academic growth, bilingualism, and biliteracy.

Students' Motivation and Engagement in Learning

Successful dual-language programs have high expectations for all students; they are provided with the support necessary to meet the expectations, and their talents and achievement are recognized on a regular basis. Whatever level of motivation students bring to the classroom is transformed by what happens in that classroom (Lowman, 1990). Factors that may contribute to increased student motivation and self-esteem are (1) interest in the subject matter; (2) perception of its usefulness; (3) general desire to achieve; (4) self-confidence and self-esteem; and (5) patience and persistence. Challenging assignments and high quality teaching helps students respond positively to well-organized instructional experiences taught by enthusiastic teachers who are genuinely interested in their students and what they learn. The activities undertaken by the program and especially by all teachers promote learning and enhance students' motivation.

Students' Academic Growth and Performance

In successful dual-language programs, grade-level (or above) academic achievement is demonstrated throughout the academic year. Even if all students do not show grade-level achievement, the school and the teacher expect that the students will make marked improvement and challenge them to achieve to their potential. Although students' grade-level performance may not show until a few years after enrollment in a program (Collier & Thomas, 2004; Thomas & Collier, 2002, 2003b), at the end of each academic year, students demonstrate knowledge and growth of content, bilingualism, and biliteracy along a continuum.

Home Involvement in Child's School Learning

Parents who are knowledgeable about the benefits of a dual-language program, and who understand its structure, tend to collaborate with the school regarding their children's education. Although some parents have a limited knowledge of the scope of their children's bilingual program, parents whose children are enrolled in a dual-language program tend to have high levels of involvement. It is crucial that parents be involved in the education of their children from the start of the program. There is a body of research that identifies the positive effect of parental involvement in children's education (Bermúdez & Márquez, 1996; Calderón & Minaya-Rowe, 2003; Carrasquillo & London, 1993; Lindholm-Leary, 2001). The spectrum of parental involvement can begin with simple parental support of the school curriculum through the reinforcement of school skills at home, to active advocacy of the program and school policies, to becoming change agents at the decisionmaking level (Calderón & Minaya-Rowe, 2003). These parents are guided, motivated, and challenged to work with their children on a regular basis, to know their children's school curriculum, and to become partners in their learning.

IMPLEMENTATION AND INSTRUCTIONAL PRACTICES

The followings steps are important to implementating of dual-language instruction.

- Development of students' sense of pride in their involvement in their dual-language instructional approach by making them aware of the merits of the two languages, especially the important role of their native language.
- Identification of the grade-level content and concepts from the different subject areas (e.g., language arts, science, art, history) that students need to learn.

- Outlining in advance the required processes necessary to achieve identified goals/standards of the specified content (e.g., inquiry processes in teaching science, emphasis of problem-solving skills in the mathematics lesson, text complexity in fiction literature in language arts).
- Listing instructional strategies and activities that teachers must use on a regular basis for challenging students in the achievement of identified goals/standards.
- Provision of appropriate contexts in which learning and teaching occur (e.g., native language is taught on a daily basis, use of interesting conversations for oral language development).
- Developing a list of classroom assessment activities to document students' work and learning growth.
- Maintenance of close contact with the parents, especially communicating the students' growth in the two languages, and their need for the enhancing and enriching of their primary language.

The delivery of the curriculum includes the development of building background knowledge, concepts, and literacy (especially reading comprehension), academic vocabulary, inquiry processes, and academic writing.

Building Domain Knowledge

Learning is the integration of new knowledge and skills with the knowledge and skills learners already possess. Prior domain knowledge is a strong predictor of a student's ability to comprehend (Shapiro, 2004) and demonstrate learning. Students will build and expand knowledge over the grade levels when opportunities are given to them to read and engage in complex informational and literary texts. It has been repeatedly said throughout this book that effective instruction activates learners' prior experience and builds background knowledge as needed. Therefore, it is crucial to activate students' preexisting knowledge so that they can relate new information to what they already know. When bilingual students' background knowledge is introduced and programmed in their first language, students are motivated to use their primary language to activate and extend information and concepts.

Teaching Vocabulary and Concepts Explicitly

Vocabulary and concept development are important components of students' domain knowledge. They serve as a cornerstone for content area learning in the two languages. Vocabulary and concepts are reflected in students' conversations, reading comprehension, and writing learning activities. What is the best way to help students master the many words they must know to understand the diversity of school texts? There appear to be two ways: (1) Teach vocabulary and concepts they need to know and (2) guide students to learn new words through reading the texts. Teaching vocabulary and concepts increases reading comprehension and domain knowledge.

One recommended strategy to enhance vocabulary and domain knowledge is to introduce words in association with conceptual knowledge: associating a new word with its similarities, differences, or relationships with other familiar concepts (Jager, 2010). For example, in a science text written in Spanish, the word *satélite* (satellite—an astronomical object that orbits a larger one) is a core word for the main concepts presented in the text. It is suggested to introduce its meaning by associating it with the phrase *Planeta Tierra* (Planet Earth), and reviewing students' knowledge of the other planets and stating that all planets have *satélites* (satellites), referring again to the planet Earth and the moon as its satellite. Science concepts introduced in Spanish (L1) may be followed by a lesson in English founded in concepts already learned in students' native language. As the students' linguistic and conceptual knowledge grows in richness and complexity, the knowledge of this concept and word label will support the meaning of the new word, which we adapted for the native languages.

Jager (2010, p. 9) recommends the following strategy:

1. Select a topic that your students need to learn. If students are below grade level, start with shorter and simpler texts, and expand them to complex domains and concepts.
2. Teach the key words and concepts directly; engaging students in using and discussing them to be sure they are well anchored.
3. As the students learn the core vocabulary, basic concepts, and overarching schemata of the domain, they will become ready to explore its subtopics, reading (or having read aloud to them) as many texts as needed or appropriate on each subtopic.

Maximizing Literacy Engagement

All teachers play a critical role in helping students think and learn with text (Vacca & Vacca, 2004; Vacca, Vacca, & Begoray, 2005). For the level of literacy needed, students must have opportunities to learn new vocabulary, continuously associating new readings with prior knowledge, adding new knowledge, discussing ideas presented in a text or by the teacher, interpreting facts and information, and applying critical thinking skills to text information. Content area texts, especially those of the social sciences and general science, are linguistically complex and densely informational, presenting historical, scientific, and technical information, for which students need to have the processes to understand and discern the information, to connect ideas, and to evaluate the information. There is an extensive body of knowledge indicating that teaching students how to use reading strategies enhances their reading comprehension (Duke & Pearson, 2002; Vacca & Vacca, 2004). Schools can significantly alleviate the negative effects of socioeconomic disadvantage by providing students with a rich print environment to become actively engaged with a diversity of literacy activities (Cummins, 2011), especially through the native language. In addition, students' access to print materials plays a role in facilitating behavioral, educational, and psychological outcomes in children, especially positive attitudes toward reading, and increasing reading performance (Lindsay, 2010).

Affirming Students' Identities

In many instances, bilingual students receive unclear messages about their cultural and linguistic differences and how these differences are valued or not valued in society, the media, their communities, and especially in school. As Nieto (2005) says, the attitudes that young people develop about their culture and heritage, and the decisions they make, cannot be separated from the social and political context in which they live. As Cummins (2011) points out, by lacking identity affirmation in the classroom, many of these marginalized students find identity affirmation on the street. He adds that schools need to challenge the devaluation of students' language, culture, and identity in the wider society and teachers need to implement instructional strategies that affirm students' identities, such as the following.

- View multicultural and bilingual students as economic resources. Teachers could talk on the strengths of students and bring case studies and instructional tasks to show that ethnic and linguistic diversity promote global and economic growth in society.
- Allow students to use their native language in and outside of the classroom, and convey the message that using the native language is an enrichment resource for learning.
- Constantly talk about the richness of the students' language and culture, and include it in the daily curriculum, content, and concepts from a variety of cultures. In addition, provide opportunities to consider concepts and ideas from different cultural and ethnic perspectives.
- Provide support beyond academics (ethnic and language clubs, ethnic sports); reinforce students' attitudes, leadership, and critical thinking by involving these students in a variety of extracurricular activities.

Checking Comprehension Frequently

Comprehension is a creative, multifaceted process in which students engage in making meaning with the content or the text. Comprehension is one of the most difficult skills to master, especially in the areas of science, math, or social studies. Students need to use their prior knowledge and experiences and the author's text to construct meaning that is useful to the reader for an identified purpose.

Initially, since bilingual students do not use the academic native language frequently, they may not comprehend informational textbooks even in their native language. Many of the books contain high levels of complex linguistic structures and concepts, which are unfamiliar to the learners. Students benefit from improved comprehension skills at all levels of native language proficiency and literacy development, which allow them to read more accurately, follow a text or story more closely, identify important events and concepts in a text, master new concepts in their content area classes, and complete classroom assignments and assessments.

Many students benefit when teachers use the following comprehension instructional strategies in dual-language classrooms.

- Provision of pre-reading activities to develop background knowledge with the topic. Teachers can use graphic organizers/charts, discussions, prediction templates, and questioning to provide students with information about the topic to be taught.
- Provision of guided reading to monitor students' use of reading comprehension strategies. It is recommended to start with short passages on the topic and subsequently add more complex texts.
- Provision of opportunities to respond to the content learned. Extensive discussions are helpful in providing main ideas and supporting concepts. In addition, writing activities to respond to the topic and its interpretations are useful in checking for comprehension.
- Provision of tasks in which bilingual students apply the content and the concepts learned—for example, students make projects to deepen their understanding of the topic, compare readings on the topic, or write reports on one area of the topic.

Extending Academic Language

As students progress through the grades, the academic tasks they are required to complete and the linguistic contexts in which they must function become more and more complex and challenging. Students are required to read increasingly complex texts in the content areas of the curriculum (science, mathematics, social studies, and literature). As Cummins (2011) mentions, "The complexity of academic language reflects: a) the difficulty of the concepts that students are required to understand, b) the vocabulary load in content texts that include many low frequency and technical words that students typically do not use in conversation, and c) increasingly sophisticated grammatical constructions (e.g., passive voice) and patterns of discourse organization that are almost never used in everyday conversational contexts" (pp. 4–5). Students are required to read complex academic language as well as engage in academic writing (e.g., reports, essays, text summaries). A recommended strategy is to teach students how to monitor their understanding, first in the native language. Students are guided to make an analysis of the language difficulty of the text and implement strategies to deal with the difficulty.

Scaffolding Meaning

The term *scaffolding* refers to the provision of instructional supports that enable learners to carry out tasks and perform academically at a higher level than they would be capable of without these supports (Cummins, 2011). Some forms of scaffolding focus on modifying and mediating the immediate input, making it comprehensible to students. Other scaffolding forms operate on students' internal cognitive structures, enabling them to develop long-term strategies for effective learning. In the native language classroom, scaffolding provides opportunities to engage learners with cognitive and challenging learning tasks, providing the support necessary for the particular demands of the learning tasks. There are a variety of representational formats (visual, oral, electronic, text) for scaffolding meaning. For students to negotiate or create meaning that makes sense based on their background knowledge, experiences with the topic and knowledge of the language structures help to convey meaning. Challenging tasks using teacher scaffolding are conducive to learning and critical thinking. In scaffolding meaning, we recommend the use of graphic organizers, questioning, monitoring, and creative thinking.

> *Graphic organizers:* Visual frames that organize information.
> *Questioning*: Frameworks for the topic under discussion.
> *Monitoring*: Checking comprehension and production, paying selective attention to specific aspects of a task.
> *Creative thinking*: Expanding the learner's point of view using the imagination to explore a whole range of activities.

USING WRITING AS A TOOL FOR LEARNING

Students need writing environments that are interactive and meaningful, as well as conducive to the development of ownership of their writing, and a purpose or reason to write (Carrasquillo & Rodríguez, 2002). At the beginning stage, bilingual students will be guided through a set of instructional strategies that they will follow when confronting a writing task (Graham & Perin, 2007) and once they become familiar with these guided activities, they will become empowered to write for different purposes and audiences on their own. For bilingual students, even though writing in their native language may not be as difficult as in the second language, as they move up the grade-level ladder, the complexity of writing increases and they need all the tools available to be able to confront the different types and levels of writing in language arts, as well as in the content areas.

Bilingual students need to begin to use writing to learn concepts, to expand ideas or content, as well as to summarize information from textbooks, from the Internet, from oral presentations, and from teachers. Bilingual students, as all students do, need to know how to take notes and to organize information by themes or topics. They need to be able to write complete and accurate sentences and paragraphs to convey learning. They also need to produce different types of writing such as narrative, descriptive, argumentative, and expository. The following list of instructional strategies (adapted from Graham & Perin, 2007) is very effective in promoting writing in the bilingual classroom.

- Give students explicit strategies/steps for planning, revising, and editing their compositions and written products (e.g., graphic organizers, brainstorming, outlining).
- Provide step-by-step formats on how to summarize information in texts or on the Internet (e.g., outlines, structure maps).
- Provide activities in which students work together, collaborating to plan, draft, revise, and edit their compositions. Students of different writing levels are mixed to allow for leadership in the conversations and discussions about writing.

- Provide opportunities to complete reachable writing tasks. The level of the tasks is increased as students show progress within the writing product.
- Use computers, iPads, and word processors as instructional support for writing assignments. These assignments may include summaries of information. interpretation of information, or expository writing such as writing a letter.
- Provide step-by-step guidelines on how to construct more complex and structured sentences.
- Guide students to generate and organize ideas for their writing.
- Engage students in analyzing information and data to develop ideas and content for writing.
- Provide students opportunities to read and analyze ideas and modes of good writing.

ONE-TO-ONE CONFERENCES

Conferences between teacher and bilingual students give learners an opportunity to share what they are learning, and they also allow teachers to help frame a student's thinking and check for understanding and level of achievement. This instructional approach works for all levels of learners with some modification of questions to meet the needs of the individual learner. In dual-language programs, the conference should be done frequently and in students' primary language, to allow them to use their strongest language to express their thoughts. For example, a conference with a student after he or she has completed a fiction reading in Spanish may include asking the following questions to guide his or her learning and understanding.

- ¿Que libro escogiste? ¿Qué clase o tipo de libro escogiste? (cuento, ensayo, novela) What book did you choose? What type of book is it? (a short story, an essay, a short novel)
- *¿Por qué escogiste este libro?* Why did you choose this book?
- ¿Habías leído algún otro libro de este mismo autor? ¿Por qué? Have you read anything else by this author before? Why?
- *¿Habías leído algún otro libro sobre el mismo tópico o tema?* ¿Habías leído algún otro libro parecido a este? Have you read a book on the same topic before? Have you read any other books that are like this one?
- ¿Te gustó el *libro? Describe el comienzo del libro. ¿Cu*ál es la parte más interesante del libro? Did you like the book? How did it start? What has been the most interesting part?
- ¿La forma en que el autor *empezó a escribir este libro, te gustaría a ti usarla para escribir algo tuyo?* Did the author begin the book in a way that you might like to begin a piece of writing?
- ¿Podrías compartir conmigo alguna sección en particular *que te gustó mucho?* Can you share with me a section that you particularly like?

A one-to-one conference is useful in different situations. For example, when a student did well on a test, the teacher can convey satisfaction with the performance.

Alternatively, when the student did not do well, the teacher may offer a plan of action to learn more. If the conference is after students have completed a learning task, the purpose is usually to check or verify students' comprehension or performance. With respect to another instructional circumstance, the conference may happen before the reading in order to help students understand and identify the organizational approach of the material, which will better prepare them to locate and organize important information that may be presented.

A VIGNETTE OF A DUAL-LANGUAGE SCHOOL

The school illustrated in this vignette is a K-8 dual-language school (English/Spanish) located in an urban area in the United States. It is part of an increasingly rich diverse community (predominantly a working-class Latino and African American community). The school enrollment is around 1,050, serving mostly low-income Hispanic students, with a 60/40 ratio of Spanish- to English-dominant speakers from kindergarten to the 8th grade. The ethnic breakdown of the school is 85% Hispanic, 8% Black, 5% Asian, and 2% White. Forty-two percent of the school population are classified as English language learners and 4% as having a learning disability. Students come from different levels of English and Spanish fluency, and from different ethnic, cultural, and socioeconomic backgrounds.

This dual-language school focuses on language and literacy development while offering an interdisciplinary cross-cultural curriculum. The school's goal is to develop fully bilingual and biliterate students, while nurturing the social, emotional, physical, and intellectual growth of its students in two languages. The students hope to not only surpass academic standards, but to also become caring, productive citizens who respect linguistic and cultural diversity. The philosophy is one of empowering students with a purposeful education and appropriate skills for an increasingly diverse, technological, and multicultural society.

All students learn how to speak, read, and write in both English and Spanish. The school emphasizes a multicultural curriculum and celebrates students' individual backgrounds and heritages. The classroom organization is not based on balancing students' first and second language, but on the assumption that by instructing and conducting school work in two languages, students will become bilingual, biliterate, and academic achievers. The teachers and administrators have developed a program that is progressive, challenging, and addresses the needs of the whole student body. The school follows a 50/50, side-by-side instructional model. The program completely immerses students in grades K–5 in both languages. On day one, a cohort of students enters a classroom where English is the only language of instruction, while on the subsequent day, that same cohort of students enters a Spanish-only classroom. A team of two teachers work collaboratively to ensure that the instruction between English and Spanish is seamless; where Teacher A stops, Teacher B picks up the next day in the other language. When attrition occurs, some teachers instruct in a self-contained dual-language classroom, whereby the teacher delivers instruction in both languages on an every-other-day schedule. At the junior high school level, a bilingual content area specialist instructs the students in both languages.

Dual language (English and Spanish) is evident throughout the entire school. Upon entering the building, the school's curriculum and the students' projects and individual work are displayed in both languages, providing a framework for the linguistic nature of the school—that both English and Spanish are spoken, written, and read throughout the whole school. The school promotes a positive and reciprocal instructional climate, and strong home/school collaboration. There is a climate of collaboration among teachers and the whole school staff. Teachers are always trying to give the best of themselves, and they are open to professional learning and its implementation.

There is an emphasis in facilitating students' development of the two languages simultaneously with curriculum support to relate content in the two languages, in both the oral and the written forms. The ultimate goal is the achievement of a balanced state of bilingualism and biliteracy. The school provides students with a challenging interdisciplinary curriculum. Recognizing that dual-language learning is about more than just language and vernacular, the school emphasizes a multicultural curriculum, celebrates the individual backgrounds of its students, and the students' academic achievement in both English and Spanish. The lesson delivery is monolingual, either in English or in Spanish, and teachers have opportunities to collaboratively develop their own units of study for literacy and content areas.

The teachers are bilingual and have an educational background in their area of specialty (e.g., early childhood, childhood, subject area) as well as certification in bilingual education. The teachers' philosophy is centered on a strong belief in bilingualism and commitment to their students' learning in two languages, development of biliteracy, and critical thinking skills. The teachers use students' cultures and experiences as resources and set up a classroom context and environment where learners are guided to take risks and become actively engaged with the new language and school curriculum. They effectively implement practices that have been shown to increase students' language and literacy development (i.e., oral language, vocabulary, reading comprehension, writing development), subject matter content, concepts, and language proficiency.

Students are eagerly engaged in learning; the school proudly reports a 97% attendance record. They do not show any concern for the "identified language of the day"—for them, it is a natural process that on Monday, all the instruction is in English and then, on Tuesday, teaching and learning is provided in Spanish. Since English is the dominant language for most of these students, some of them speak in English with their peers during personal communications on Spanish days, but once the teacher is in control of the class, Spanish becomes the language of communication, with some code-switching in each language.

The students' overall academic performance is above average, compared to similar schools in the area, with the added advantage that this school's students are developing bilingualism, biculturalism, and biliteracy, demonstrating learning and academic achievement.

The following variables have contributed to the successful implementation of dual-language instruction:

1. The administrative staff has created a school culture in which bilingualism, biliteracy, and cross-cultural understanding and involvement are important indicators in teaching and learning. The school radiates a sense of pride in

being or becoming bilingual and biliterate. This positive attitude toward bilingualism is transmitted to all, including the parents, teachers, school staff, students, and the community. There is a demonstrated collaboration of all the school personnel toward helping students become successful bilingual learners.

2. Teachers believe in the bilingual program and in bilingualism. They understand dual-language instruction, and plan collaboratively with other grade teachers to provide high-quality content and instruction in the identified language of the day. Content, skills, and instruction provided in English and Spanish share the same high-quality level. Teachers feel comfortable and motivated to make their students bilingual, biliterate, and academically successful learners.

3. The school has implemented a well-developed core curriculum program that includes the separation of the two languages for instruction and using the teachers' strongest language for instruction.

CLASSROOM ASSESSMENT OF BILITERACY GROWTH

One of the key elements in dual-language programs is the development of a process for obtaining academic information about students' growth, especially in the area of biliteracy, which is proficiency in understanding, speaking, reading, and writing in two languages. It is important to determine the level and rate of acquisition and proficiency in both languages as well as the grade level of reading comprehension. The implementation of this assessment process is systematic, multidisciplinary, and closely related to individual students' instruction for the purposes of producing information about students' conceptual, linguistic, and cognitive development. The assessment of biliteracy growth is a cyclical process, as illustrated in Figure 5.1.

Figure 5.1. Assessment of Biliteracy Growth: A Cyclical Process

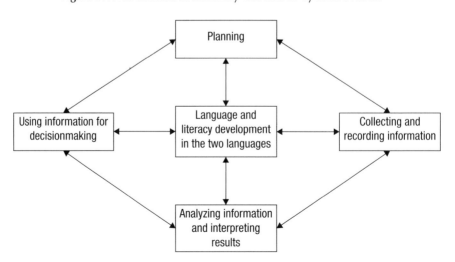

It is important to use multiple tools continuously and over a period of time. O'Malley and Valdez Pierce (1996) recommended that the assessment of literacy should include these characteristics: (1) be based on activities used to teach reading and writing; (2) measure decoding, fluency, and reading comprehension skills; and (3) be conducted regularly, and on an ongoing basis. Two recommended tools are a literacy growth portfolio and a student language and literacy profile. The literacy growth portfolio collects authentic students' data over a period of time, and if summarized appropriately, it can present an objective overview of students' performance and development. The classroom language and literacy profile summarizes test data providing information on individual students' performance in comparison with other students that match their grade level and curriculum expectations.

Collecting Students' Growth in Literacy Through a Portfolio

The literacy growth portfolio is a purposeful collection of a student's work documenting his or her efforts, progress, and achievement in a given area. A learner's performance is evaluated in relation to instructional goals, objectives, and classroom activities. The information collected represents the level of the student's performance within the curriculum, including the identified learning standards. This information is useful for these reasons: (1) describing the educational developmental levels of each student; (2) describing specific qualitative strengths and weaknesses in students; (3) identifying the extent to which the student has attained the prerequisites needed to go into new or advanced learning; (4) describing commonalities about students; (5) describing students' performance with respect to specific targets; (6) providing feedback to students about their level of performance; and (7) providing feedback to parents about their child's progress toward learning goals. The information generated helps teachers in modifying their instructional approaches and strategies to better meet students' linguistic and academic needs.

The portfolio includes various kinds of information (e.g., poems, narratives, tape recordings, retellings, literature responses, reading comprehension tasks, observations, and writing samples) that indicate the student's progress. It also includes observations, checklists, anecdotal records, interviews, and classroom tests. Figure 5.2 describes these various classroom assessment tools and illustrates how they can be used to yield useful information for the portfolio.

Although the portfolio is not the main assessment tool for assessing students' academic and biliteracy level, it documents information on the bilingual and academic journey of students participating in dual-language programs. The portfolio can be used subsequently for multiple purposes, including instructional planning. The outline illustrated in Figure 5.3 lists key information to include in a portfolio.

Student's Language Characteristics and Strengths

Individual students' experiences with language and print must be examined to determine academic starting point and growth. This examination must be based on students' language background and proficiency levels. For example, it is important for educators to know what language group a child represents (e.g., Chinese [Cantonese

Figure 5.2. Classroom Assessment Tools

Tools	Tool Description
Oral interview	Students respond orally about a range of topics that help teachers to identify students' prior knowledge; past experiences related to language and literacy; and their interests and preferences.
Observations	Through observations, the teacher can gain insights into students' knowledge about sounds, meaning, and syntax, and their capability to speak and interact appropriately in different situations.
Questioning	Questioning helps to identify bilingual students' level of experiences and background knowledge about topics and concepts.
Anecdotal records	These are brief, written descriptions of concrete actions or events observed by the teacher (e.g., notes, record situations that describe how students are progressing in the use of academic vocabulary in Spanish language arts).
Story or text retelling	Retelling a story or reporting informational text in the students' own words requires thinking about the story that was read or told; relating events of the story; and arranging the events in sequence.
Checklists/Rubrics	These are sets of key behaviors that typically represent an activity of interest or a phase of literacy development and identifying markers of developmental levels within the set of identified behaviors.
Writing prompts	These prompts provide clear information about the student's writing performance and level of proficiency and growth, revealing, for instance, whether students use writing strategies to gather and organize ideas; whether they use feedback from teachers and peers and whether they think about their audience when they write.

or Mandarin], Spanish, Burmese, Haitian Creole, Russian), and be able to describe and document the experiences and knowledge of each bilingual student in the native language and in the second language. In identifying students' language strengths, the results of the *Home Language Survey* may provide knowledge on initial identification of the dominant or stronger language, and to identify individual learners' weaknesses and strengths in both languages that will be helpful in planning for instructional decisions.

Student's Level of Native Language Development

The student's level of language acquisition in the primary language must be determined. In addition to school data, the teacher can consider interviewing the parents about their child's first language in open-ended and structured formats to determine the parents' beliefs and expectations about their child's language level. Knowledge of parental experiences may be compared with peers who speak the same native language. This analysis may show that the student may be in the process of acquiring an oral foundation in the native language, and that he or she is in the process of developing literacy in the native language, which is encouraged by their parents at home.

Figure 5.3. Portfolio Outline

I. Student's Information

Student: _____ Age: _____ Grade: _____
Student's L1: _____ Student's L2: _____ Years in Dual-Language Programs: _____

Add a picture of the student with a short autobiography, signed by the parent/caretaker. (Give students a choice of language in writing his or her autobiography.)

II. Teacher's Assessment of Student's Language Characteristics and Strengths

Include one/two paragraphs presenting a brief description of student's language level, needs, and strengths

   a. Native language development
   b. Student's level of proficiency in the second language

III. Parent Short Interview

Parent will be interviewed to present a perspective of child's home language emphasis and his or her perception of the dual-language long and short-term goals related to the child/student.

Tell me a little bit about the language used by your child at home, in church, with his or her friends. Which is his or her preferred language for communicating with you? Why? What are you doing at home to help your child to become bilingual?

Dígame algo sobre la lengua/el idioma que su hijo usa en la casa, en la iglesia o con sus amigos. ¿Cuál es el idioma preferido de su hijo? ¿Por qué? ¿Qué tareas está haciendo Ud. en la casa para ayudar a su hijo a ser bilingüe?

IV. Examples of Student's Work Demonstrating Listening, Speaking Development in _____ (e.g., Spanish, Cantonese, Korean, Bengali) (Written in chronological order, the most recently completed one is the first one to include.)

   a. Oral interviews
   b. Classroom observations
   c. Checklists
   d. Retellings
   e. Audio recordings
   f. Others

V. Examples of Student's Work Demonstrating Reading Development in _____ (e.g., Spanish, Cantonese, Korean, and Bengali) (Written in chronological order, the most recently completed one is the first one to include.)

   a. Reading summaries
   b. Reading comprehension tasks
   c. Literature tasks
   d. Vocabulary exercises

VI. Examples of Student's Work Demonstrating Writing Development in _____ **(e.g.,** Spanish, Cantonese, Korean, and Bengali) (Written in chronological order, the most recently completed one is the first one to include.)

   a. Examples of writing demonstrating multiple modes (narrative, descriptive, expository, opinion)
   b. Rubrics
   c. Creative writing

VII. Teacher's Brief Summary of Student's Development/Progress

Identification of Student's Proficiency in the Second Language

In general, schools assess bilingual students' proficiency in the second language (usually in English) through standardized proficiency tests. Teachers may want to add additional tools to vary standardized data. When developing a plan to assess student's first and second language proficiency and literacy, teachers may want to start by outlining major instructional goals or learning outcomes, matching these goals to learning activities, and identifying assessment tools (e.g., observations, writing samples, comprehension charts) to collect information on the student's strengths and growth.

Student's Knowledge of the Structure of Both Languages

It is also appropriate to assess what learners know about the structure and form of the two languages. This is usually done through an interview or a written language sample. Areas to assess may include the complexity and length of sentences; frequency and complexity level of academic vocabulary; and knowledge domain and complexity level of oral language.

Student's Daily Language Use

An interview with the students or their parents/caregivers is useful in identifying the type of language the students use on a daily/regular basis. The teacher should also observe and start writing observations on students' use of the two languages. Observations may address the following questions: (1) When and why do students use their native language?; (2) When and why do students use the second language?; (3) What language do they use primarily with their peers?; and (4) What linguistic strategies do students use when they are forced to speak the "weak" language?

Student's Language Curriculum Demands

Educators should examine and describe the language skills students need in order to fully participate in the dual-language program. Is the program presenting language arts in both languages? Is subject area content provided in one or in both languages? Which academic vocabulary is promoted in L1 and L2? Are students following the school curriculum or is it a simplified curriculum? What is expected from students at the end of the school year? Answers to those questions help teachers identify the language demands of the program on each student. Conferences with students and their parents are encouraged.

A CLASSROOM LANGUAGE AND LITERACY PROFILE

The *Classroom Language and Literacy Profile* provides an overview of a classroom's performance in standardized and curriculum-based tests. By examining the whole class's level of performance and the achievement gaps of subgroups, educators can customize instruction to attend to the whole class, to classroom subgroups, and to individual student needs. Figure 5.4 provides an example of a dual-language classroom literacy profile.

Figure 5.4. Language and Literacy Profile

Academic Year _____ School _____
Class _____ Teacher _____
Grade _____

Student	L1	L2	English Proficiency & Literacy Scores						Spanish Proficiency & Literacy Scores					
			SPEAKING		READING		WRITING		SPEAKING		READING		WRITING	
			Oct.	June	Oct.	June	Oct.	June	Oct.	June	Oct.	June	Oct.	June
Dual-Language Program	Sp.	Eng.	B/I/A	B/I/A	B/I/A	B/I/A	B/I/A	B/I/A	B/I/A	B/I/A	B/I/A	B/I/A	B/I/A	B/I/A
Colón, Carlos	L1	L2	B	B	B	I	B	I	I	A	I	I	I	I
Díaz, Petra	L1	L2	B	B	B	B	B	B	A	A	A	I	I	I
Flores, Marta	L1	L2	B	I	B	I	B	I	A	A	I	A	I	I
Gómez, Ines	L2	L1	A	A	A	I	I	I	B	I	B	I	B	I
López, Juan	L1	L2	B	I	B	I	B	I	A	A	B	I	I	I
Martín, Iris	L2	L1	A	A	I	I	I	I	B	B	B	I	B	I
Negrón, Jose	L2	L1	A	A	I	I	I	I	B	B	B	I	B	I
Ortiz, Patricia	L2	L1	A	A	I	A	I	B	B	B	B	I	B	I
Pérez, Digna	L1	L2	B	B	B	I	B	I	B	A	B	I	I	I
Reyes, Arturo	L2	L1	A	A	A	I	I	I	B	B	B	I	B	A
Santos, Maria	L1	L2	B	B	B	I	B	I	B	I	I	A	I	I
Soto Lydia	L1	L2	B	A	B	I	B	I	A	A	I	I	I	A
Viruet, Emma	L1	L2	B	B	B	I	B	I	I	I	B	I	B	I
Vargas, Angel	L2	L1	I	I	I	A	I	A	B	I	I	I	A	I
Zayas, Ariel	L1	L2	B	B	B	I	B	I	I	A	B	A	A	I

Value of Scores: B/Beginning: 0–20%; I/Intermediate: 21–60%; A/Advanced: 61% and over
Source: The format of this profile was developed by A. Carrasquillo and the New York City Bilingual Education Training Center (BETAC).

The following steps make use of the tremendous amount of assessment information provided through both the individual literacy growth portfolio and the language and literacy profile.

- Periodically combine the material in the portfolio into a form that can be used in conferencing with staff and parents when communicating with them about the child's language and literacy strengths, as well as instructional needs and support.
- Meet with family and staff to present assessment information stressing the level of student growth and development.
- Use the information to plan instructional strategies and identify goals for moving students along a continuum of growth.
- Use the information to inform curriculum development and implementation, appropriate to a particular student's level and needs.
- Due to the fact that the portfolio consists of an extensive amount of different types of information, a rubric or a checklist needs to be developed to analyze and summarize the data.

Promoting Native Language Instruction in the Special Education Classroom

Se não houver luz	(If there be no light
Vou amar-te em Braille	I will love you in Braille
Ou	or
Escrever com dedos ousados	write with daring fingers
Em alfabeto jamais usado	in an inaugural, exclusive
Único	alphabet
Que escorra em nossas peles,	that flows over our skin as truths,
verdades	tunics, guides.
Túnicas, Guias	Ours is the possibility of breaking all
Pois somos donos da possibilidade de	the staffs,
quebrar	of reinventing the sun and the magic
todas as bengalas	of the days.)
De reinventar o sol e a mágica dos dias	

(Juan Carlos Limeira, 8th grade student, "Mágica")

(translated by Bruce Dean Willis, University of Tulsa, "Enchantment")

As communities in the United States continue to become more culturally and linguistically diverse, more bilingual learners with and without disabilities are present in K–12 student populations. This demographic change in student populations calls into question the extent to which past and still present instructional methods and assessments are appropriate. There is a broad literature describing the benefits of teaching bilingual students with disabilities in their primary language (Bowman-Perrott, Herrera, & Murry, 2010; Freeman & Freeman, 2008; Rodríguez, 2009). The studies show that these learners need differentiated and supportive academic instruction, and a familiar language to facilitate learning and academic development. In many instances, educators are pressured to immerse students in English, and do not promote teaching and learning in the students' primary language. Yet the use of the primary language facilitates the provision of academic content, as well as instructional and learning activities. These students also need the provision of social learning to enhance their intellectual and social growth, in addition to adapting to a new culture and a new language. Adapting to a new culture is very complex and stressful, especially when one must learn a new language. A bilingual learner with a disability or disabilities must resolve how to retain her or his own original identity while being bombarded with new expressions and customs.

This chapter provides an overview of issues relevant to the cross-cultural dynamics of classroom instructional settings in K–8 schools, suitable adaptations for the development and implementation of an appropriate curriculum, and effective teaching strategies for fostering literacy development and knowledge domain for bilingual students with disabilities. The chapter lists challenges and strengths of bilingual learners (BLs) with disabilities, providing insights into the question of which language should be used for instruction, in addition to describing effective learning environments and instructional considerations for teaching and learning. The chapter ends with a brief summary of principles to follow when assessing bilingual learners with disabilities.

The chapter attempts to provide answers to the following questions: (1) How does federal legislation provide the framework for the provision of appropriate instructional contexts for bilingual students with disabilities?; (2) How do appropriate instructional environments and strategies meet the academic needs of bilingual students with disabilities?; (3) Which language should be used for instruction?; and (4) What provisions should educators use in the assessment of bilingual learners with disabilities?

BILINGUAL LEARNERS WITH DISABILITIES: THE LEGISLATIVE INSTRUCTIONAL CONTEXT

The first federal law prohibiting discrimination on the basis of disability was passed in 1973. Section 504 of the Rehabilitation Act of 1973 prohibited the denial of services to individuals with particular disabilities in programs or activities that receive federal financial assistance. But inadequacies in the legislation required additional measures to ensure equality for individuals with disabilities. In 1975, the Education for All Handicapped Children Act (EAHCA) was passed, which was renamed the Individuals With Disabilities Education Act (1990) 15 years later, with revisions in 1991 and in 1997. The current Individuals With Disabilities Education Improvement Act of 2004 (IDEA) establishes a strong message on equality of educational opportunities for all learners.

Although federal legislation impacts schooling, education in the United States is largely under state jurisdiction. Additionally, the right to an education for children and youth is a matter of state law and implementation of educational laws are a matter of state legislation and funding. Another consequence of state jurisdiction over education is that federal protection against discrimination in education is often limited to programs and activities that receive federal financial assistance and may ignore the six principles in implementing appropriate programs and assessment for students with disabilities: (1) free appropriate education; (2) least restrictive environment; (3) an individualized education plan; (4) nondiscriminatory evaluation; (5) due process; and (6) universality of application. Fortunately, as Hoover, Klingner, Baca & Patton stated (2008), IDEA takes "precedence over state law, such as proposition 227 in California (teaching bilingual students in special classes that are taught mainly in English), so it is appropriate to use native language instruction for students with disabilities in states with English only policies" (p. 62). An additional national law protects bilingual students with disabilities: Title II of the Americans with Disabilities Act (1990) prohibits discrimination on the basis of disability by all public entities. IDEA 2004 provides for a diversity of disability categories (e.g., intellectual/learning disability, developmental delay, emotional disturbance, autism, and deaf-blindness). The biggest group is within the category of learning disability.

EFFECTIVE LEARNING ENVIRONMENTS

Bilingual learners with disabilities are able to learn and to contribute to the social and cultural environment if they are given meaningful opportunities to connect their school learning with their home learning. In a favorable sociocultural learning environment, learners' cultural and linguistic strengths are integrated into the teaching and learning process and in the school environment to foster cognitive and social growth. The most effective learning environment for bilingual students with disabilities is a community of learners (Baca & Cervantes, 2004), in which the teachers set high expectations when planning, developing, and implementing instruction. The environment enables teachers to advocate for bilingual students with disabilities to help ensure equal educational access rights and educational opportunities that include their culture and language. In essence, teachers affirm, accept, and respect the identities of their diverse students and become active contributors of community integration. Instruction is based on students' strengths, using native language skills and ability, cognitive/intellectual ability, and degree of disability. This is how teachers foster effective learning and, in turn, help students become citizens who contribute positively to society, entail knowledge, and a level of human independence. Education is key to success, and regardless of learners' disabilities, students finish school, get married, have children, work, and pay bills. In other words, these students are seen as capable of making positive contributions to society. Educators connect the school, family, and community dynamics to the educational experiences of students with disabilities. The result of an effective educational environment and teaching is shown in Figure 6.1.

Figure 6.1. Educational Environment

Contributions to Society

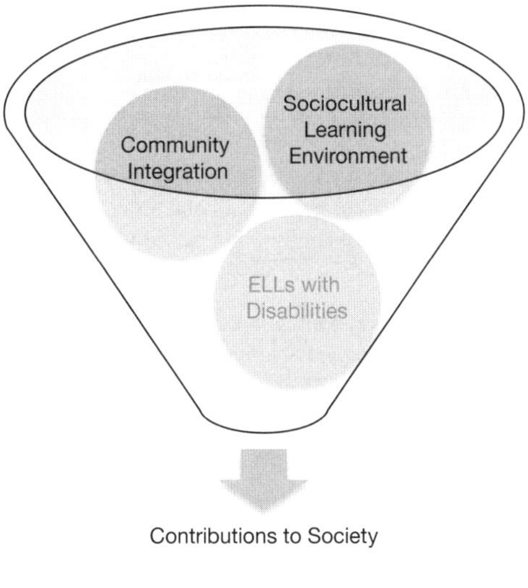

BILINGUAL SPECIAL EDUCATION

Bilingual special education is the instruction of academic content in two languages (English and native language) with a specifically designed program to meet the needs of children and youth who are acquiring a second language and who have a disability (Baca & Cervantes, 2004; Haagar & Klingner, 2005; Zhang & Cho, 2010). Educators need to examine each student's degree of disability, level of intellectual/cognitive ability, and level of language proficiency in English and the native language. The biggest challenge for educators in the field of bilingual special education is institutionalizing the practice of language support in the academic program fostering bilingualism and multiculturalism. Once the program is institutionalized at the school level, appropriate instruction, materials, and resources are made available as well as support for bilingual teachers and other resource staff.

Bilingual special education is conceptualized as the basic paradigm of instruction in specialized educational settings in two languages. Bilingual learners with a disability who are instructed in two languages (the native language and English as a Second Language) must be identified, evaluated, assessed in the two languages, and provided with an individualized educational plan for both languages with accommodations for the disability. Even though culturally and linguistically diverse students are overrepresented in special education classes in comparison to the total population (Artiles, Kozleski, & Waitoller, 2011; Kea, Campbell, & Richards, 2004; Klingner, 2004), many of these students do not receive an equal and appropriate education due to the lack of appropriate programs, especially bilingual ones.

Three terms are usually used in the literature to identify bilingual students with disabilities. Figure 6.2 lists and describes these terms.

Bilingual students with disabilities are entitled to an appropriate education and an individualized education plan that addresses their language and cultural characteristics and proficiency. When developing an educational plan for bilingual learners with disabilities, educators (particularly the multidisciplinary team) must be knowledgeable about concepts such as language development, native language, and second language

Figure 6.2. Bilingual Special Education Terms

Terms	Definitions
Bilingual learners with disabilities	Students with a physical, mental, or developmental impairment whose native language is not English, they participate, attend, and learn in bilingual educational settings, and usually demonstrate dominance in the home language.
Emergent bilinguals with disabilities	Children and youth with a disability, who are at the initial stage of English language proficiency and demonstrate dominance in the native language.
Culturally and linguistically diverse (CLD) learners with disabilities	Children and youth with a disability who are raised in a language and culture other than English; may or may not be fluent in the English language; may or may not show fluency in the home language.

acquisition. These educators, especially teachers, need to provide an array of instructional materials, resources, and strategies in the student's strongest language, which in most cases is their native language. If appropriate instruction is not provided, these students will be subjected to inappropriate services. These students need appropriate language support to develop the academic, linguistic, social, and affective domains of learning. Enrolling these students in bilingual special education programs ensures educational opportunities through specially designed instruction and related services to meet their unique needs, which enables them to achieve on a level commensurate with their abilities.

José and Pedro: Bilingual Learners with Disabilities

The following two vignettes of José and Pedro illustrate the diversity within the field of special education.

> José Rodríguez did not begin speaking until he was 3 years old. He always had difficulties with communication at school and at home, often remaining withdrawn and unsociable. He was even removed from school at one time because of his emotional instability. José's test scores are well below average except for his performance on creativity measures. With respect to creative tasks he shows some potential. Other than reading intently and playing a musical instrument, José seems to have few interests and expresses little personal or vocational goals. José's parents are of Latino descent, with high school education.

> Pedro Rosario has never spent much time in school. He started late because of an illness and was withdrawn several times due to continued sickness. Pedro has been labeled "backward" by school officials. He has suffered from a variety of ailments and is going deaf. Although his creative performance shows some promise, Pedro's IQ score is low (81), as are his scores on other achievement indices. However, Pedro enjoys building things and mechanical pursuits, has good manual dexterity, and would like someday to be a scientist or railroad mechanic. Although Pedro's mother is well educated, she does not speak English. His father has had no formal schooling and is unemployed.

To some extent, these two vignettes provide part of the biographical background information of Albert Einstein and Thomas Edison, but are included in the chapter to raise the following questions: (1) What type of instruction do José and Pedro need?; (2) Would you expect them to fit in within a regular class program?; (3) Would they benefit from native language communication and instruction?; and (4) What language strategies would you use when teaching these students? The answers to these questions lead us to identify the talents, skills, and strengths of students with disabilities to enhance and promote successful educational outcomes and opportunities to learn.

Also consider these important questions regarding the identification of the strengths and needs of Pedro, José, or any other student with a disability: (1) Is the Individual Educational Plan (IEP) in the language that the parents can understand and read?; (2) Is the IEP culturally sensitive?; (3) Is the IEP presented in a continuum of the academic progress of the student?; and (4) Is the bilingual learner with a disability on the academic track or on a vocational track? Educators, along with the parents, must be advocates for each bilingual learner with a disability or disabilities. The IEP should address the role of sociocultural background, language proficiency in the native language and in English, and the cognitive/intellectual ability of the learner. Partnerships among school administrators, community organizations, teachers and parents establish positive relationships of effective and successful bilingual special education classrooms and contribute to appropriate teaching and successful learning.

WHICH LANGUAGE SHOULD BE USED FOR INSTRUCTION?

When selecting the appropriate language of instruction for bilingual learners with disabilities, Hoover and Collier (1985) recommend consideration of these questions:

(a) What is the student's native language?; (b) What is the student's English level of proficiency?; (c) What is the student's most proficient language—English or the native language?; (d) What native language instructional resources are available?; (e) What English language instructional resources are available?; (f) Does the student's IEP specify language of instruction; and (g) If not specified in the IEP, what is district policy for selecting language of instruction? (p. 16)

Once the language for instruction is identified, programmatic instruction is planned, developed, and implemented. Planning includes determination of appropriate academic content based on multiple factors, including cultural environment and students' prior background knowledge, as well as students' linguistic abilities and degree of disability.

The language for instruction is also determined by school philosophy and parents' decisionmaking. In a bilingual special education program, the native language and the second language (English) should be the two selected languages for instruction. The native language serves as the foundation language. Typically, literacy and content areas are taught initially in the native language and the second language is gradually introduced into the curriculum. This approach helps students acquire the second language, maintain the native/primary language, and progress through the academic curriculum. Hamayan and Damico (1991) stated that the "level of proficiency that students have attained in their native language at the time they began to learn the second language directly affects how easily and effectively they will attain proficiency in the second language" (p. 50). The use of a variety of instructional strategies, along with modifications and adaptations, facilitate this dual-language approach. For example, the use of the native language for instruction provides natural oral interaction between peers in large and small groups through projects, collaboration in activities, demonstration and modeling of correct language use, and active participation in experiences that stimulate language development in a spontaneous way.

The use of complex language for authentic purposes, providing opportunities for language to be infused into the learning experience (to ask questions, experiment with language, and make mistakes), is part of the bilingual instructional plan.

The following list identifies strategies for the development of concepts, processes, and skills in the bilingual special education classroom. All of the strategies help students synthesize knowledge by considering, describing, retelling, and/or writing about experiences and concepts. Instructional strategies may include

Translations	Drawing	Note Taking
Cognates	Classifying Concepts	Pictures
Audiovisuals	Technology	Think-Alouds
Hands-on Activities	Explicit Vocabulary	Games
Graphic Organizers	Conceptual Mapping	Acting
Using Books on Tape	Modeling	Brainstorming
Demonstrating	Reciprocal Teaching	Storyboards
Story Maps	Concept Mapping	Free Writes

When planning, developing, and implementing instruction, teachers should regard, confirm, elaborate, and consult (Herrera & Murry, 2007). First, teachers should ensure that the instructional strategy is appropriate and effective for the bilingual learner with disabilities; second, that the instructional strategy provides multiple ways of learning the content; and third, that the collaboration is provided for the educational well-being of learners. Valle and Conner (2011) believe that planning a lesson is an art of "crafting an interactive, engaging environment in which students learn and demonstrate knowledge about what the teacher has predetermined and what has not been predetermined" (p. 108). A thoughtfully planned and executed lesson includes the writing of well-formed objectives enabling scaffolds and adaptations, as well as modifications to fit the learners' linguistic and academic needs and strengths, including the learner's native language strengths. For example, through use of the cognates as shown in Figure 6.3, students can draw on prior knowledge in the native language to learn words in other languages. This activity enhances their understanding of language in learning. Students can also use synonyms to enhance their own learning.

Figure 6.3. Cognates

English	Spanish	Portuguese	Haitian Creole
Describe	Describir	Descreva	Dekri
Define	Definir	Defina	Defini
Analyze	Analizar	Analise	Analize
Evaluate	Evaluar	Avalie	Evalye
Apply	Aplicar	Aplique	Aplike
Clarify	Clarificar	Esclareça	Klarifye
Connect	Conectar	Conecte	Konekte
Interpret	Interpretar	Interprete	Enterprete
Compare	Comparar	Compare	Konpare

Vygotsky's (1978) notion of the "zone of proximal development" indicates that favorable learning conditions exist when students are stretched beyond their current developmental level. In the bilingual special education classroom, this is accomplished through scaffolding that supports academic, linguistic, and social learning. The following vignette, written by a teacher in a college course on teaching bilingual learners with disabilities, illustrates classroom "favorable learning conditions" used by an ESL teacher in using students' native language and cultural background.

Every student does not learn the same way, and every student comes to us with unique experiences to share with us in the classroom. I learned to fill out a biography card to help me understand where students are from, what their schooling was like, and what they know. This would help me to provide a more smooth transition for them. I also incorporate more about other countries into my teaching since it is something students are familiar with and experienced. It would also benefit my other students who are from other countries as well. I make sure that I let students speak, read and write in their native language. One thing that I have learned is to keep those students together, they need to continue to socialize using their first language; use of their first language also provides them comfort and helps them learn the English language over time.

(Heidi Smith, ESL teacher, New York)

Heidi Smith's story illustrates that establishing connections between the new content and the learner's experiences is made much easier when the teacher takes into account the student's native language, interests, cultural background, prior knowledge, and disability.

Teaching reading comprehension in the native language facilitates the process of using syntactic, semantic, and rhetorical information found in printed texts, to reconstruct, in the reader's mind, knowledge of the world using cognitive skills and reasoning ability (Cummins & Swain, 1986). This process provides a link between what was taught and what was learned, and teaching and learning become an interactive process, developed gradually through a process of acquisition and acculturation of cognitive, cultural, sociolinguistic, and communicative skills. Connections are established between the ideas in the passage and the learner's own personal experiences, including activities that involve topics and experiences related to what the student has nearby. Students are curious and want to discover information that will enhance their lives. For example, the following teacher reflection narrative illustrates a strategy to introduce vocabulary in bilingual students' strongest language using scaffolding strategies. The narrative includes a reference to a vocabulary quilt, which is illustrated in Figure 6.4.

One instructional method that I use in the classroom is the vocabulary quilt. I have used this activity with all classes that I have taught. I have students create a quilt individually, and they write important vocabulary words in each box. Students then write everything they know about the word. This includes definitions, pictures, and examples. Students use their preferred or strongest language to complete the activity. In the second part of the activity, students go into groups to share their vocabulary quilts with their group members. Students discuss what they have in their quilts and why they have it. Students then take their quilts and make a giant quilt using chart paper. Students work together

Figure 6.4. A Vocabulary Quilt

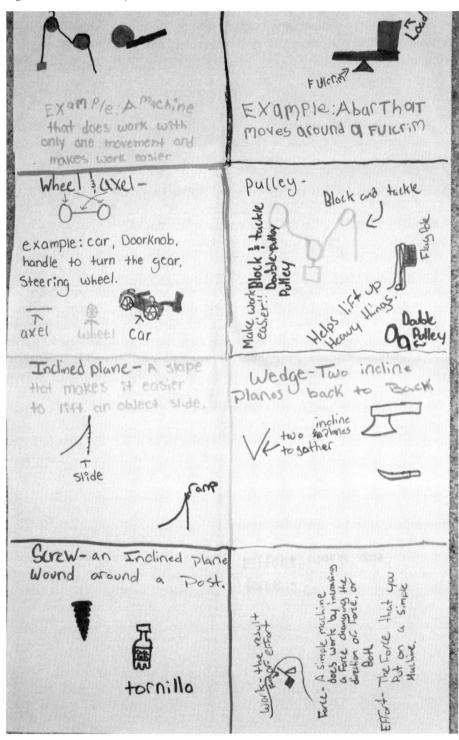

Drawing by Amanda Reilly.

to complete the quilt based on what the group has synthesized. Then student groups present their quilts to the class to share their understanding. This activity allows students to use academic vocabulary while talking with other students. It also allows bilingual learners with disabilities to share their first language, which makes them successful at contributing by helping nonbilingual students learn new culture and language from bilingual learners with disabilities.

(Amanda Reilly, ESL Special Education Teacher, New York)

All the above information illustrates that bilingual learners with disabilities will benefit by the use of the native language as the initial language of instruction, and gradually incorporating instruction in English.

Teaching Language Arts in the Students' Native Language

The instructional needs of bilingual learners with disabilities vary according to the learner's cognitive/intellectual ability, language proficiency in English and the native language, and the degree of disability. Ortiz (2001) recommends the identification of effective strategies based on the learner's prior knowledge, concepts learned, practice opportunities, connecting the curriculum across content areas, filling academic gaps, and maintaining a positive connection with students. Effective teaching includes the following: (1) adapting or developing materials that are culturally and linguistically appropriate; (2) instructional strategies correlated with the student's learning style and level of disability; and (3) continuous monitoring of the student's level of engagement and response to the instruction provided. Figure 6.5 provides an example of a language arts lesson taught in the native language of a Haitian student.

This lesson provides an opportunity for each student to think about their own name and participate in a cognitive activity, the writing of a poem, which involves multiple activities (e.g., thinking, reading of the words, choosing the appropriate words, writing) to attain the learning goal. Familiarity with the Haitian Creole language would make this high-level cognitive activity interesting and easier for bilingual students with disabilities.

Teaching Domain Content Knowledge

One of the most difficult instructional challenges in the bilingual special education classroom is to teach domain knowledge and concepts. We strongly suggest using students' strongest language, use of appropriate content materials, and motivating instructional strategies. Teaching content and concepts effectively includes the following:

- Providing an atmosphere that is conducive to articulating different points of view;
- Using the native language (or students' strongest language) to link the general school curriculum so that students have the language foundation for acquiring in-depth knowledge of the content;
- Modeling during content-oriented discussions to elaborate the concepts learned;

Figure 6.5. Haitian/Creole Language Arts Lesson

The purpose of this lesson is to teach 3rd-grade students that their name has a special meaning; and to use the first letter of their names to capture the essence of their name.	Plan lesson sa ap ede w anseye elèv ke non yo gen siyifikasyon espesyal epi kijan yo ka sèvi ak chak lèt non yo kòm premye lèt nan yon mo ki kaptire sans non yo. Langaj 45 Min Kl s: 3 ane / ELL Entèmedyè Avanse
Objective	**Objektif**
After reviewing adjectives describing personal attributes, students will write an acrostic poem about their name.	Apre nou fin revize adjektif diferan ki dekri atribi pèsonèl nou, elèv la ap ekri yon powèm akrostich sou non yo.
Introduction	**Entwodiksyon**
Teacher asks students what makes someone special; what makes each student special. Teacher shares an example of an acrostic poem about a special person.	Pwofesè ap mande elèv yo kisa ki fè yon moun espesyal Pwofesè ap mande kisa ki fè chak elèv espesyal Pwofesè yo pral pataje yon egzanp yon powèm akrostich sou yon moun espesyal
Procedures	Aktivite
Tell students that they will be writing a special poem about themselves; everyone is special and unique. Give students word banks or brainstorm words of interest on the board. Have several words to choose from, to facilitate the writing of the poem. Make an ABC word list on a poster and have students include as many words as possible on the list. Have students write their name horizontally. Have students write a sentence or phrase beginning with each letter of their name using the word list. Have students work in pairs; revise draft; publish the final draft.	1. Di elèv yo ke yo pral ekri yon powèm espesyal sou tèt yo paske tout moun espesyal ak inik. 2. Bay timoun yo bank mo, oswa réfléchi mo enteresan sou tablo a 3. Pare lis plizyè mo ke elev yo ka chwazi pou yo ekri powèm lan 4. Fè yon lis mo ABC sou yon afich epi fè elèv yo mete otan mo ke posib nan lis la. 5. Di elèv yo ekri non yo an orizontal. 6. Fè elèv yo ekri yon kòmansman fraz oubyen yon fraz ak chak lèt nan non yo lè l sèvi avèk lis mo yo. 7. Pèmèt elèv yo travay ak yon lòt moun pou sipò kanmrad. 8. Edite epi revize bwouyon powèm la. 9. Fè elèv pibliye vesyon final la, epi ilistre lipou plezi.
Assessment	**Evalyasyon**
Did students complete the poem? What was the level and appropriateness of the words they worked with?	Elèv yo ap evalye sou jan yo fini powèm lan, ak itilizasyon adjektif ki apwopriye.

Compiled by Nathalie Cajuste, Miami Dade College.

- Integrating appropriate technology to provide opportunities to learn new materials using a variety of instructional devices (technology tools, language, and content level must be appropriate for the students with disabilities);
- Using grouping configurations (e.g., total group, small groups, partners, one to one) to assist learners as they examine and discover new content area concepts;
- Providing opportunities to interact, participate, and answer throughout the lessons by drawing, writing, or even translating; and
- Continuous monitoring of students' engagement and interest during lesson implementation.

The following teacher reflection provides an example of how to use students' strengths and native language in teaching the science concept of the water cycle to a group of bilingual students with disabilities.

The water cycle is a process that happens in nature all around us. I taught the water cycle to the whole classroom group over the course of two weeks using books, a song, experiments, and putting on a reader's theatre. I explained: "Today we would be working in small groups creating a Water Cycle Bracelet to use it in retelling the stages of the water cycle." I used the overhead to display the graphic organizer of the water cycle bracelet. I showed the students how to construct their bracelets by using the same materials they had on their tables. Students were then divided into small groups; each table had the materials necessary for beginning the project. Students had to color in the graphic organizer according to the water cycle stage. I circulated around the room listening to student conversations about what each colored bead represented on the bracelet as each student made one. I asked questions such as (1) Rain, sleet, and snow are all types of what? (2) Which bead represents precipitation? (3) When water evaporates, where does it go? (4) Can we see evaporation? Why/Why not? (5) Are clouds water? In what stage of the cycle do clouds form? I videotaped a small group discussing their activity, and asked them to orally retell the water cycle. The visual cue cards and graphic organizer helped as they were retelling the cycle. The students actively engaged in a hands-on activity, creating a water cycle bracelet using visual cue cards, and through oral retell were able to understand the journey water takes each day. The Water Cycle activity allowed students to orally retell the water cycle using the bracelet as a visual reminder. The students used their native language to retell the stages of the water cycle giving them more confidence and better understanding.

(Wendy Burke, ESL teacher, Florida)

Critically important to teaching in the content areas is the writing of educational objectives for each student with disabilities. How are teachers and the multidisciplinary team writing those instructional objectives? What kind of modifications and adaptations are implemented and delivered throughout the teaching? When will teachers set up meetings with parents to discuss accommodations for bilingual students with disabilities? Is there a plan for intervention and evaluation for the learners? Are the teachers taking into consideration the acculturation, learning style, culture, language, experience, and disability in designing appropriate educational objectives? Have the teachers considered the language of instruction for these children and youth with disabilities? Teachers must consider ways of monitoring meaning through the implementation of the objectives and provisions for modifications and accommodations. For example, are the bilingual learners with disabilities given testing accommodations in their native language? Are bilingual learners with disabilities given accommodations associated with test-taking, time, presentation, and language?

ASSESSING BILINGUAL LEARNERS WITH DISABILITIES

Assessing students with disabilities presents a challenging task due to the variations in disability (e.g., hearing impaired, learning disability, behavior disorder, speech/language disorder) and the lack of appropriate instruments for testing the bilingual student. One of the main concerns of educators is current assessment practices in school districts, including use of appropriate instruments and methods for assessing bilingual learners with disabilities. Most of the assessment instruments that appear to work with monolingual students are useless with bilingual students with disabilities, since they were not developed for this population. Baca and Cervantes (2004) pointed out that satisfactory assessment must describe the following: (1) student's biography; (2) academic context; (3) interaction between the learner and the academic context; (d) students' weaknesses and difficulties; (4) proposed alternative educational agenda/plan to ensure the success of the learner; and (5) repertoire of teaching strategies for the student.

Bilingual learners with disabilities have needs and strengths that must be considered when assessing language proficiency in order to determine the language for instruction as well as a plan for academic and social growth. These students are better assessed using a continuum for rating scales and authentic assessment tools, which reflect real, meaningful, and relevant life tasks that require reading, listening, speaking, and writing. Student self-assessment samples should also be included in assessments. Regarding reporting, appropriate assessment includes a summary of the student's language, cognitive, and academic strengths, as well as a description of the mastery level of the native language and the second language. Valle and Conner (2011) recognized that the assessment must be "student-centered, activity based, and product oriented" (p. 161). A key source of information for assessing the progress of a student is the teacher who observes the bilingual learner coping with a variety of academic demands in class, and who can provide accurate information on the student's academic and linguistic strengths and instructional needs. The following example, which continues the teacher's reflection on teaching the concept of the water cycle, provides insights into continual classroom assessment of bilingual students with disabilities.

My students' language proficiency and academic achievement are based not solely on a formative weekly assessment, but through oral reports, presentations, demonstrations, written assignments, and portfolios. For example, I assess the progress of beginner bilingual students by asking them to label a picture or diagram, to draw a picture that demonstrates a key idea, to explain an idea orally, to answer a few questions orally, and to submit a project in lieu of an in-class test. I decided to use these hands-on approaches in assessing my students' understanding of the water cycle for the following reasons. I have students working in cooperative groups. The peer interaction that takes place during cooperative learning activities is especially helpful because peer language is generally less complex than the teacher's. These interactions also give all students a chance to actively participate and try out their own ideas in a small group setting. I observe them, make notes of the oral interactions and I write comments about their level of engagement and conceptualization. Their portfolios are a display of work they performed during and after the individual lessons.

(Wendy Burke, ESL special education teacher)

Assessing bilingual students with disabilities must include the child's development in the first language as well as their academic progress made through the identified language of instruction. Student progress is evaluated along a continuum, which provides a measure of how much progress students have made in a given time period, rather than the standardized measurement of grade-level curriculum and learning standards. The level of disability and the individual educational plan provide the foundation for considering a student's academic and linguistic progress.

7

Using Bilingual Students' Native Language in the Content Areas

Today is the first day of school for many immigrant children,
anxious parents bringing their precious ones to school
hoping that they possess the proper clothing and school supplies.
Parents are hopeful that their children will learn and relate with peers from
America and from all over the world.
From Taiwan, Russia, Bangladesh, Mexico, Kenya, and perhaps Haiti.
Although they look different, parents are hopeful they can cope
with the new school, the new language and the different teachers.
All everyone wants is to learn, to get good grades and a diploma.
Will there be many anxious, fearful and nervous new students?
Will there be opportunities to be able to make friends?
Will their grades be as outstanding as they were before?
So many students, a rainbow of cultures and languages.
Instead of fear and anxiety, this first day will go smoothly,
students and teachers will greet each other shyly
with a warm smile, communicating HOPE and LEARNING.

(Angela Carrasquillo, "The First Day of School")

Content area instruction provides students with opportunities to explore and acquire knowledge, concepts, and skills in a variety of domains, which include social science, sciences, and mathematics. Students' content and conceptual knowledge acquisition is a developmental process from K–12 and becomes more specialized at the college level. In the last few decades, content area instruction has undergone major philosophical and instructional shifts revolving around the conceptualization of integrating language and content, building knowledge, providing opportunities for increasing conceptual and linguistic complexity, inclusion of complex informational texts and literary texts, and emphasis on academic content vocabulary (Duguay, 2012; Echevarria, Vogt, & Short, 2010; Short, Fidelman, & Louguit, 2012). For bilingual students, these philosophical emphases support the use of the students' strongest language in the acquisition of domain knowledge, concept skills, and academic vocabulary. Teaching students in their primary language makes sense for learning subject area content because bilingual students have the linguistic and literacy foundation to master grade-level knowledge and literacy.

This chapter provides an overview of the theoretical and instructional conceptualization for teaching subject area content, skills, and processes in students' native language and for the integration of content and language, especially in the subjects of mathematics, social science, and sciences. The chapter attempts to provide answers to the following questions: (1) What strategies are useful for providing students opportunities to integrate language and content?; (2) What are the instructional steps teachers should follow when using background knowledge and vocabulary development in the content areas?; (3) What is the rationale behind teaching the content of mathematics, social studies, and science in the students' native language?; and (4) What are the instructional and learning advantages of using thematic content approaches?

INTEGRATING LANGUAGE AND CONTENT

The bilingual education literature highly recommends the integration of native language and content during instruction (August, Artzi, & Mazrum, 2010; Carrasquillo & Rodríguez, 2002; Snow, 2005) because doing so gives the students opportunities to continue to learn and grow academically and cognitively while acquiring academic language (Duguay, 2012; Echevarria & Graves, 2003; Grant & Lapp, 2011; Sherris, 2008). Language is not just a medium of communication but it is also a vehicle to learn content across the curriculum, and to build literacy skills, especially reading and writing. Cognitive skills are global across the disciplines (e.g., understanding cause-effect relationships, hypothesizing, making inferences), and learning language and content can be presented as an integrated systems process. The emphasis and complexity of content and language vary at different times within a topic, unit, and lesson. Fluency and accuracy in all four language skills (listening, speaking, reading, and writing) are used in the context of content-relevant tasks, and in the service of building mastery of a body of content knowledge.

New curriculum trends, likewise, promote the integration of language and content. For example, the national Common Core State Standards movement recommends that educators, especially teachers, emphasize the following areas: (1) balancing informational and literacy texts; (2) domain knowledge of the disciplines; (3) provision of a staircase of complexity; (4) inclusion of text-based answers; (5) writing information based on a diversity of sources; and (6) promoting academic vocabulary. In planning for the integration of language and content, two main areas require further discussion: the role of students' background knowledge and the building of content academic vocabulary.

ROLE OF BACKGROUND KNOWLEDGE

The complexity and diversity of information covered in the different content areas (i.e., science, social sciences, and mathematics), combined with the difficulty of understanding content area texts, leaves teachers with the responsibility to build students' background knowledge before the beginning of content lessons. It is common to find bilingual students who are unfamiliar with some of the conceptual information reflected in the content area lessons due to the fact that the lesson includes components that are unfamiliar to the students. Carrasquillo and Rodríguez (2002) found that building bilingual students' background knowledge facilitates making connections between new information and prior knowledge and provides a bridge to understanding new content: What is learned is based on what is already known. Background knowledge strategies are used to introduce new content, knowledge, and concepts in order to tie new content back to the students' preexisting knowledge and personal experiences (Carrasquillo & Rodríguez, 2002; Peregoy & Boyle, 2005). Figure 7.1 lists components or factors addressed in the development of new concepts and domain knowledge in the native language classroom.

Introducing background knowledge in the teaching of content areas helps to motivate and facilitate the comprehension of particular concepts and domain knowledge (Echevarria & Graves, 2011). For example, using brainstorming at the beginning of the lesson encourages students to share what they already know about the topic, and connects the content to their personal experiences. Figure 7.2 lists examples of activities that are useful for building background knowledge in preparation for a content lesson.

These examples reflect ways for teachers to create meaningful learning situations that build on previously acquired knowledge.

BUILDING CONTENT VOCABULARY IN THE NATIVE LANGUAGE

Bilingual students are continually challenged to expand and build on their content vocabulary. Therefore, time needs to be set aside for vocabulary building before delivery and after each lesson. Students must be able to determine word meanings, identify the function of words (e.g., noun, adjective), and steadily expand their repertoire of words and phrases, particularly ones important to academic discourse. Students expand their vocabularies through conversations, direct instruction, reading extensively and writing on topics about different experiences. Vocabulary knowledge involves

- Knowing the meaning of words, including multiple words for the same related concepts: *coraje, ira, furia* (anger, enrage, inflame).
- Knowing multiple meanings, both common and uncommon for a given words: *"Estoy con mucho coraje, ira, furia."* ("I am very angry, enraged, inflamed").

Figure 7.1. Development of Domain Knowledge

Factor	Conceptualization
Academic Language	Vocabulary knowledge, complex syntax, structures, academic discourse.
Vocabulary	Discipline-specific words necessary to understand main concepts of the lesson.
Comprehension	Understanding of the information and main concepts.
Communication	Ability to share information and points of view.
Engagement	Involvement in instructional activities designed to facilitate acquisition of particular knowledge, skills, or capabilities.

Figure 7.2. Activities for Building Background Knowledge

Activity	Examples
Brainstorming on main concepts	"What do you know about the concept?" "¿Qué sabes de las hojas de los árboles?" ["What do you know about leaves?"]
Starting with basic concepts	"I am sure that you know about the four seasons. Let's list them." "Let's rewrite what we already know about the seasonal changes in trees."
Developing related ideas	"When I was coming to school this morning I noticed that leaves have many colors and many of them are falling. Why do you think this is happening?"
Drawing from students' personal experiences	"How many of you have tried to help your mother or father clean the yard of all the leaves?" 여러분 중에 몇명이나 마당에 있는 모든 낙엽들을 치우기 위해 어머니나 아버지를 도와드리려고 한 적이 있습니까? ["Have you observed more leaves on the ground?"] 당신은 땅위에 있는 모든 낙엽들을 보기위해 최근에 공원에 가본 적이 있습니까? ["Have you gone to the park lately to see all the leaves on the ground?"]
Bringing multiple genres to domain knowledge and concepts	"Do you remember the story that we read several weeks ago about the *Giving Tree*?" "Let's briefly summarize the message of a short book that we read."

Figure 7.3. Building Background Vocabulary

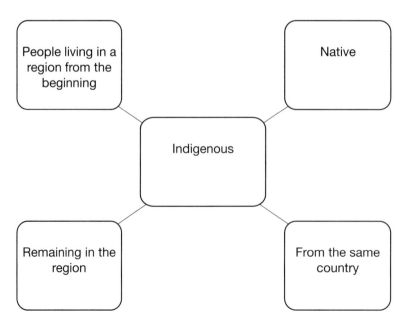

People living in a region from the beginning

Native

Indigenous

Remaining in the region

From the same country

USING GRAPHIC ORGANIZERS TO BUILD VOCABULARY

A graphic organizer is a useful strategy to build native language academic vocabulary. These organizers (e.g., semantic maps, webs, diagrams, or any cognitive organizer that engages students in a mental activity) provide students with visual illustrations related to concept building and word definitions. These visual illustrations activate prior knowledge, providing multidimensional contextual clues to add new words and new knowledge to students' communicative and receptive language. The conceptual graphic organizer in Figure 7.3 takes the academic word *indigenous* and provides known words to facilitate the establishment of meaningful relationships.

PREPARING STUDENTS FOR A CONTENT LESSON

One of the most important recommendations for teachers is the preparation of a list of steps to follow when preparing students for a lesson. The steps in Figure 7.4 are useful for motivating and preparing students for a content area lesson, in this case a lesson on photosynthesis. The following example addresses the topic of photosynthesis again because it is an important concept at all grade levels of the science curriculum: early childhood, middle grades, and high school.

Although the example is provided in English, bilingual teachers will apply these principles using students' native language.

THEMATIC APPROACHES TO TEACH CONTENT AREAS

The use of thematic approaches is a helpful method to introduce content knowledge that relates to other areas of the curriculum. This approach engages bilingual students in activities in which they use their native language in meaningful contexts and in new complex ways. Thematic approaches allow instruction to incorporate a variety of language concepts, content, and cultural activities. These activities allow students to be active participants in tasks that require them to negotiate meaning, reflect on their claims, and practice language to acquire content knowledge while advancing toward literacy and biliteracy (García, 2005)

The "theme" of the curriculum should connect with a thread of related concepts and activities that links different subject areas. Content in one subject area is integrated with different areas of the curriculum, exposing students to a variety of texts and perspectives. Students will complete different types of comprehension experiences and write pieces for different purposes and audiences. Vocabulary is enhanced through investigating topics embedded in the content, which is informed by myriad perspectives. As shown in Figure 7.5, learning becomes a more fluid and interrelated cognitive process: Students read, write, and think about content, while simultaneously building language, literacy, and domain knowledge.

Figure 7.4. Steps to Prepare Students for a Lesson on Photosynthesis

Area	Early Childhood	Middle Grades	High School Grades
Concept Objectives	Understand the role of light in the process of photosynthesis. Observe the effects of light on plants.	Identify the parts and functions of plants. Identify the source of food of plants; understand the process of food and matter transformation.	Understand photosynthesis as a process used by plants. Understand the relationship between photosynthesis and cellular respiration.

Recommended Steps	Activities for Early Childhood Grades	Activities for Middle Grades	Activities for High School Grades
Building students' background knowledge	Ask students the question "What do you think of when you hear the word 'plant'?" While students respond to the question, their answers are recorded in a KWL chart.	Provide three different types of plants for students to observe in groups. Answer through a graphic organizer: "How do plants help us live?"	Interview a partner prior to the lesson, to find out about his or her country's environment and foliage; and share three pieces of information.
Vocabulary words	Roots, stem, seed, leaves, oxygen, air, soil, water, photosynthesis	Chlorophyll, photosynthesis, oxygen, carbon dioxide	Photosynthesis, chlorophyll, cellular respiration, stoma
Teaching core vocabulary or terminology in advance of new content	Conversation to identify the parts of a plant and the related vocabulary; say statements using the words.	Draw a plant; identify, and label parts of the plant. Using a concept map, define vocabulary words (energy, sunlight, water, oxygen, and carbon dioxide)	Provide students a list of words with sentences attached; read, discuss, and define the words; add a sentence to each word.
If the textbook has the content-specific vocabulary identified, review the words.	Using the word *oxygen*, discuss "Who needs oxygen? What is the symbol for oxygen?"	Review words before the lesson to help students match words and definitions.	Identifying words, and creating definitions.
Provide the content information.	Use pictures to describe the photosynthesis (process).	Watch a short video about photosynthesis.	Watch a short video about photosynthesis.
General questions to be answered	"What are the main parts of a plant?" "How do plants grow?" "What do plants need to grow and to become strong?"	"Where do plants get their energy?" "How do plants use energy to produce food?" "What do plants need in order to produce food?"	Describe the relationship between photosynthesis and cellular respiration. "Why are stomata an important part of photosynthesis?"

Figure 7.5. Themes to Connect Different Content Perspectives

Unit Topic: How are countries adversely affected by earthquakes? How was Haiti adversely affected by the earthquake?

On January 12, 2010, Haiti had an 8.1-magnitude earthquake that adversely affected the entire country. Houses, schools, and government buildings were destroyed or damaged, and the country's commerce, health, education, and living conditions were tremendously beaten by the earthquake.

Research Stage

Students will work through a variety of activities, including demonstrations, group collaborations, individual information searches, lectures, and video observations in order to prepare a report on one of the following areas:

Social Sciences	Arts, Music, and Literature	Science	Math
General overview of Haiti	*Haitian lifestyles*	*Haiti's latest earthquake information*	*How did the earthquake affect Haiti in the following ways?*
• Geographic information • Language • Ethnic background	• How do Haitians express themselves in music, art, and literature?	• Damage • Intensity	• Housing • Health • Education • Economy

Learning Activities to Engage the Students

- Prepare a map indicating the geographic location of Haiti, its capital, and main cities. Using a map scale and cardinal directions, identify the land that was affected by the earthquake.
- Prepare a comparative table indicating the population of Haiti before and after the earthquake. Supplement the table with reasons for the increase or decrease in population.
- Write a research paper on the cause of earthquakes.
- Write a letter to a Haitian student expressing solidarity with them for the sorrows caused by the earthquake.
- Prepare a selection of art, music, or literature from Haitians that express their feelings toward the devastation and subsequent demonstration of survival and rebuilding skills after the earthquake.
- Organize a panel to discuss how people need to prepare themselves for the arrival of an earthquake in their area.

The following steps are helpful in the conceptualization and implementation of a thematic unit.

1. Identify a relevant theme that is included in the grade-level curriculum to motivate students using a guided inquiry. Example: "Creemos que las plantas son importantes para toda la gente, y así se indica en la unidad que debemos estudiar. ¿Cómo las plantas facilitan la vida del hombre?" "We believe plants are important to all people, and the unit that we will study emphasizes this, but think about, how do plants facilitate the life of men and women?"
(" 우리는 모든 인간에게 식물이 중요하다는 것을 알고 있고, 우리가 배울 단원도 이 점에 대해 강조하고 있는데, 그렇다면, 식물이 인간의 삶을 과연 어떤 식으로 용이하게 하는지에 대해 생각해 봅시다.")
2. Include a planning stage: Brainstorm the content to be studied and consider the types of information and strategies necessary for the development of the unit. Clearly articulate a conceptualization of what needs to be done by both students and the teacher. The planning stage includes information gathering from multiple sources (e.g., texts, articles, newspapers, Internet); communication with subject area teachers; constant feedback; and reflection.
3. Provide an initial set of resources and identify a list of other resources, complete with information about how to find them. Tools that students use for manipulating instructional materials must be accessible to them (e.g., computers and Internet connections).
4. Assist students with compilation and analysis of content. The process of compiling information from several sources and analyzing the information puts considerable language/literacy demands on the students.

A Theme to Investigate a Topic of Interest

While teachers and students are involved in a particular lesson, a topic may arise that becomes of interest to participants, even though it is not part of the identified curriculum. The teacher may use this opportunity to explore the topic and address students' interests. This enrichment activity may provide opportunities to culturally analyze information from different perspectives and domains.

A Thematic Unit

A theme is used to organize the grade-level curriculum by integrating multiple disciplines, including reading, mathematics, sciences, social science, and the arts around a broad topic such as "communities," "rain forest," or "weather changes." Themes provide students with interdisciplinary learning through (1) effective use of technology; (2) increasing student engagement; (3) use of collaborative/cooperative learning; (4) focusing on clear objectives; and (5) providing students with opportunities to conduct investigations, which include gathering and analyzing information.

INTEGRATING CONTENT KNOWLEDGE AND LITERACY IN MATHEMATICS, SOCIAL STUDIES, AND SCIENCE

Content Domain Knowledge: The development and expansion of information, concepts, processes, skills, and dispositions acquired through a combination of experiences and education.

Language and Literacy: Ability to read information, ability to write coherently, and think about the writer's world. Literate learners have expanded vocabulary, and are able to associate new reading to prior knowledge, as well as interpret facts and information, and understand all forms of communication.

The content area curriculum provides learners a wide variety of learning experiences, materials, and instructional strategies to accommodate a broad range of individual differences as well as learning needs and interests. It also requires involvement of learners' thinking, reasoning, decisionmaking, and problem-solving abilities. The following sections provide a brief rationale for teaching subject-specific content in the students' native language and include examples of recommended instructional activities to guide teachers.

Learning Mathematics in the Native Language

Mathematics learning has a primary focus in the school curriculum. The rationale for teaching mathematics in bilingual students' native language is that mathematics content goes from simple conceptualizations and operations to higher contextualization greatly dependent on language. Algebra, as well as other mathematical courses, presupposes understanding of language skills and literacy. Students cannot attain proficiency in mathematics without understanding the language in which the mathematics is exposed (Association of Latino Administrators & Superintendents, 2011). Mathematics is an important component of cognition: the ability to think, to reason, and to solve problems. Mathematics instruction for bilingual students needs to consider students' literacy level and mathematics knowledge in order to provide experiences that bridge gaps in mathematics literacy, and prepare them for success in future mathematics course work and experiences (Carrasquillo & Rodríguez, 2002). The native language is the best language to teach students' conceptualizations and operational skills. Learners have the language and literacy foundation necessary for comprehension, analysis, and solving problems. We recommend teaching and learning mathematics in the native language since the native language provides (1) required language background for understanding content, influencing meaning, and predicting context; (2) familiarity with complex sentence structures; (3) familiarity with mathematics academic vocabulary; and (4) knowledge of basic mathematics concepts.

The native language provides opportunities for regular and active participation in the classroom—not only when reading and listening, but also when discussing, explaining, writing, representing, and presenting content and concepts. Content and process of mathematics include:

- Constructing meanings;
- Solving problems in meaningful situations;
- Using thinking strategies to learn basic facts;
- Integrating mathematical concepts to the other content areas;
- Introducing mathematical concepts to students in real-world situations;
- Developing awareness of number sense; and
- Understanding the relationships between operations.

Recent curriculum trends put a great emphasis on teaching mathematical operations as well as the appropriate use of mathematics' language (Aguirre-Muñoz, 2010; Association of Latino Administrators & Superintendents, 2012). For example, curriculum experts propose that teachers emphasize language focus, coherence, fluency, deep understanding, application, and dual intensity.

Learning Social Studies in the Native Language

Social sciences or social studies represent content and concepts from several disciplines such as history, geography, anthropology, sociology, political science, and economics. Bilingual students' knowledge bases increase as a result of learning a body of information and concepts from all the above disciplines, in part by drawing upon relevant interdisciplinary sources. Conceptual integration is based on human interactions and leads to the integration of disciplines, language, and content. To accomplish this integration, students need to use a variety of cognitive skills such as the following: (1) understanding of cause-and-effect relationships; (2) comparing and contrasting; (3) collecting, analyzing, and interpreting data; and (4) hypothesizing and making inferences. Effective teaching of the social sciences improves students' understanding of domain knowledge, expository text, academic vocabulary, and academic universal concepts and understanding.

Reading is an important tool to build knowledge in the social studies classroom. Bilingual students need to have a strong literacy background to be able to do the following:

- Comprehend, interpret, and communicate historical facts;
- Understand domain-specific concepts;
- Evaluate intricate arguments;
- Synthesize complex information; and
- Understand descriptions of events and concepts.

Writing is the vehicle students use to convey social studies content, which reveals how they have interpreted content and applied it in different contexts. The goal is to guide bilingual students to complete multiple steps, as follows:

- Gather information and evaluate sources;
- Analyze sources in a clear and cogent manner;
- Draw justifiable conclusions based on analyses; and
- Produce high-quality written arguments in support of conclusions about the topic.

Learning social studies involves a great amount of expository readings, filled with abstract concepts, and unfamiliar names and events. Therefore, bilingual students will use the foundation they have in their native language to learn content and concepts, and to extend their critical thinking skills. Learning in the native language provides students the tools to manipulate, apply, and expand language in order to increase the knowledge of concepts and facts (Carrasquillo & Rodríguez, 2002).

Learning Science in the Native Language

Science is fundamentally an attempt to describe and explain the world; it is a way of understanding the world through multiple activities: (1) observable patterns; (2) application of discovery patterns through observation; (3) testing of hypotheses; (4) designing and carrying out experiments, including the measurement and analyses of data; and (5) synthesizing scientific information to derive justifiable conclusions and generalizations. In order for students to be able to advance in science understanding, they need an adequate level of scientific literacy, which is the ability to use scientific knowledge to question, hypothesize, conduct a disciplined investigation, and draw evidence-based conclusions in order to understand and help make decisions about the natural world and make changes through human activity to the natural world more predictable (Brown & Ryoo, 2008; Douglas, Klentschy, Worth, & Binder, 2006; National Research Council, 1998). Through the use of the native language, bilingual students are able to understand the different kinds of scientific content in texts; communicate about science; and acquire and analyze relevant science information to understand the world through observable patterns, and test hypotheses by carrying out experiments.

The literature indicates that providing science instruction in bilingual students' native language increases the language and cultural competence of the learners, and at the same time, enhances students' science learning and literacy (August, Artzi, & Mazrum, 2010; Lee, Maerten-Rivera, Penfield, LeRoy, & Secada, 2008). Benefits of using the native language include the following: (1) better recall of prior knowledge for reading and writing when engaged in scientific activities; (2) better use of prior academic vocabulary to expand science concepts and scientific literature; and (3) more opportunities for overall concept development. Fradd, Lee, Sutman, and Saxton (2002) and Amaral, Garrison, & Klentschy (2002) provide evidence that when content instruction allows bilingual students to use a variety of representational formats, such as the provision of learning materials in the native language, their content knowledge and achievement increase. August, Artzi, & Mazrum (2010) stated that teachers should implement science activities in the following manner:

- Promote comprehension of science information by interactive questioning;
- Focus on language functions for describing, explaining, reporting, and drawing conclusions in the context of science inquiry; and
- Explicitly teach and reinforce key vocabulary terms, making students aware of the need to know these words in order to make sense of the science information.

Teachers make use of appropriate instructional strategies and varieties of strategies in order to facilitate understanding of content. Those strategies facilitate learning by providing bilingual students opportunities to clarify, verify, monitor, memorize, reason, and practice new knowledge. Students need to listen, speak, read, and write through the development of the science language.

8

Technology in the Native Language Classroom

Shiksha hoti bahut zaroori
Isse dikhegi duniya poori
Man laga ke padhan seekho
Kitabon main cheezein
dhoondho.
Maa baap ko batlayo
Aaj tumne kya kya seekha
Aakhir shiksha hai aise hi
cheez
Roz seekho ge nayee nayee
cheez
Shiksha hoti bahut zaroori

(Ayan Kavimandan,
3rd-grade student, "Education")

(Education is most important
You will see the whole world
through it,
You must learn by heart
As you will find lots of
things in books,
As you find them, share them
with your parents.
Share with them what you
learned today.
After all, this is what
education is.
You will learn new things
everyday
Education is most important.)

(Translated by Shabina Khalid Kavimandan,
Kansas State University)

After more than 30 years of innovation in information and communication tech-nologies, bilingual learners and all other students must be able to use technology for learning and creative expression (Resnick, 2012). Technology is a major resource in all types of educational settings, and teachers need to know how to select, adapt, and use a wide variety of technological tools in their teaching, much of which occurs in classrooms. Technology facilitates teaching and provides students with more oppor-tunities for learning, discovering, and for creative expression, and teachers should continually explore methods and activities for integrating these tools into all areas of the curriculum, including those in the bilingual classroom and in the students' native language.

Instructional technology enhances student motivation and academic achievement, and technological devices are effective as long as schools provide the appropriate tools, teacher training, and the time needed to incorporate them effectively into teaching. Further, many teachers also recognize that learning to integrate instructional technol-ogies effectively into one's teaching practice is a journey, requiring patience, ingenuity, and creativity (Luterbach, 2013). As teachers become increasingly aware of how to use the numerous technological resources available to them, they will gain the confidence necessary to use a variety of technological resources in their teaching.

This chapter presents a framework for the use of technology in the native language classroom; it describes technology as an important learning and teaching resource, and recommends instructional activities useful for enhancing bilingual students' primary language and knowledge of the curricular content areas. This chapter provides answers to the following questions: (1) What roles do technologies play in the native language classroom?; (2) How can the use of technology meet the demands of bilingual learners in a culturally and linguistically diverse society?; (3) How does the use of technology enhance bilingual students' language comprehension and achievement in the school curriculum areas?

TECHNOLOGY IN A LINGUISTICALLY AND CULTURALLY DIVERSE SOCIETY

Through the use of technology students can engage in instruction that promotes communicative and interactive learning (Luterbach, Rodriguez, & Love, 2012; Sessoms, 2008). Due to technological advances, people throughout the world communicate using multiple technological methods and digital networks, which facilitate applications such as electronic mail, instant messaging, social networking, and even video conferencing. Bilingual students must be able to participate in this ubiquitous interconnected world of communication in order to enhance their learning environments and productivity. Sessoms (2008) eloquently stated, "As current social trends require citizens to be more analytical thinkers and to synthesize information, current teaching practices must develop these higher order thinking skills" (p. 87). Indeed, the use of technology in bilingual classrooms is imperative for the benefit of the learner and the facilitation of instruction by teachers. In today's technological society there are multiple language tools that can be used for teaching two languages in the classroom.

Interconnected communications are very common in much of the world today, including the United States, where many technological innovations continue to be developed. Technology skills are almost embodied in most young learners' lives. After all, the term *netizens* (denizens of the Internet) was developed after repeated observations of life over the past 20 to 30 years. Students are motivated to use technological devices for everyday living, which involves engagement with social media, use of the Internet, interactions with video games, and communication by chatting and texting, for instance. Imagine the benefit to bilingual learners who utilize digital communication devices in their daily lives for communication in two languages. As educators, we should make use of these technological devices in the classroom setting and beyond to encourage communication in two languages.

Numerous Internet-based companies have integrated programs that encourage students to communicate with each other in constructive and protected ways. These programs allow some students to be more comfortable expressing themselves and sharing personal information than they would be in a traditional classroom setting where a teacher would moderate such communication. These programs provide some insights into the need for educators to encourage student use of information and communication technology (ICT), especially to convey the value of communication in its different forms, including oral and written.

Since technology is part of the fabric of life in the 21st century, use of technology in today's classroom is of heightened importance. Technology continues to evolve and to be a way of daily living in society for many activities, including learning and instruction. The learning environment plays a major role in the education of bilingual learners. We are promoting the use of two languages for instruction in the classroom and the use of technology to communicate and learn in two languages, which enhances and facilitates the academic learning of bilingual students.

On a cautionary note, of significant concern to teachers and school administrators today is how safe technologies are for teaching. A technology that may appear to be useful in the classroom may not be safe for students' use. Clearly, not all technologies, websites, for instance, are safe. Educators must evaluate instructional technologies to ensure that there is no risk in using them in the teaching and learning process.

TECHNOLOGY IN THE NATIVE LANGUAGE CLASSROOM

The use of technology in the native language motivates many bilingual learners to improve academic learning. Many students use technological devices in daily life, and educators should take advantage of the technology and integrate it into everyday classroom life, especially for fostering practice in two languages. The advantage of using the student's strongest language for learning is that it expands the learner's knowledge base, including vocabulary, syntax, critical thinking, technology skills, second language acquisition, and reasoning skills.

Krashen's (1982) theory on second language acquisition provides an excellent rationale for the use of native language through technology. Krashen carefully explains how the comprehensible input hypothesis is necessary for communication and learning. In particular, he regards natural communicative input as a key ingredient for bilingual student success. In light of Krashen's hypotheses and evidence of the effectiveness of instructional technologies, we consider technology integration in the native language classroom to be important for the development of two languages for bilingual learners. Further, Sessoms (2008) affirmed, "Teachers that create interactive learning environments must be equipped with both technical skill and an integrated pedagogy with technology as the foundation" (p. 95). Taking into consideration features of effective learning environments, we strongly recommend the use of technology to teach in two languages. The U.S. Department of Education (n.d.) stated that with proper design, technology can easily represent information so that there are multiple alternatives, multiple options for unfamiliar vocabulary or syntax, and even alternatives to language itself (use of image, video, and audio). With innovative and creative thinking, teachers can use technologies with bilingual students to foster learning of native language, English language, and content knowledge. Edwards et al. (2002) concluded that use of technology in two languages brings great advantage because the "opportunity to use two languages allows bilingual learners to develop their metalinguistic awareness: the fact that word order differs from one language to another; that different languages are sometimes written in different directions; that equivalent words in different languages often bear no physical relationship to each other" (p. 68).

TECHNOLOGY: A TEACHING AND LEARNING RESOURCE

Technology has many implications for teaching in two languages. With appropriate planning and implementation of technology tools and resources, instruction for bilingual learners in their native language and English can be effective and motivating. Villa (2002) explained that the use of technology in the classroom opens the door for native language instruction. Imagine the opportunities available to young learners who leverage their first language to learn another language while acquiring content knowledge. By the time those learners graduate from high school they will have become literate in two languages, mastered numerous technology skills, and possess content knowledge and skills in mathematics, science, and social studies. Offering such a challenging curriculum will enable bilingual learners to become critical thinkers and creative problem-solvers. Such knowledge and skills are in great demand in our 21st-century global society.

Constructing a multifaceted learning environment that integrates teaching with technology will increase learner motivation and academic effectiveness, thereby diminishing the struggles that many bilingual students face in a monolingual and monocultural school environment (Villa, 2002). In general, most children and youth know very well how to engage with technological devices and are entirely willing to do so. Accordingly teachers should seek to capitalize on their students' familiarity with technologies. Technology interconnects with language teaching and serves to mediate learning for language development (Chapelle, 2003). Bilingual students are often measured by how well they learn the language of instruction and communicate using it. By encountering content in two languages, at times through technologies, bilingual students develop additional cognitive links to images, sounds, and words in their daily activities. Effective use of technology in the classroom can help students enhance their knowledge and use of the two languages. In today's society, many learners are inclined to use technologies to learn content, which promotes reading and writing and linguistic development. To understand language, we must understand the concepts and ideas represented within; use of instructional technologies fosters such understanding.

What types of technological devices are useful in the classroom? There is such a diversity of devices, including graphing calculators, smart phones, iPads, tablets, laptops, desktop computers, and SMART Boards. Mobile devices and SMART Boards have received much attention recently. Whereas learners can easily transport mobile devices, SMART Boards are computers installed in classrooms, which permit computer-learner interactivity. The teacher and students can run software on the SMART Boards that will respond to their input. Further, teachers can join communities of SMART Board users to increase their knowledge about uses of SMART Boards and to access lessons already prepared for use on SMART Boards. The following teacher reflection provides insights into the benefits of using SMART Boards.

SMART Boards are incredible. As an educator, making flipcharts is time consuming, but it pays off. The students are excited to learn and see what the lesson entails. The lessons are interactive and allow ample opportunities for all types of learners to comprehend the topic. I can recall a lesson with a 3rd-grade reading class. The lesson was on main idea. We began by reading a short passage. Then a question geared toward finding the main idea was posed. A student was selected to come to the SMART Board and choose the correct answer. If the student chose correctly, we would hear the applause sound and the students then all joined in.

(Emily Bodkin, New York teacher)

The next teacher reflection indicates how the use of technology motivates students and provides them with opportunities to experience success.

My guided reading group consists of 1st-grade students, all of whom entered my group reading on a level 1. One of them (Shan) failed to participate in any of the group discussion. When it was time for our reading group to read their material Shan would stare off into space, make inaudible noises, or even worse, throw his book down on the ground repeatedly just so he could go to the floor to retrieve it. As the rest of my guided reading group moved up in their reading levels, Shan remained on level 1.

In introducing the lesson I did my usual introductory tasks but at the end I said I had a special surprise. I showed them the iPad. I explained to the group that Shan would be in charge of the iPad and that we needed an iPad to help us look up the words that were unfamiliar to us. I then showed the students how we would find the definition of the words. The look on Shan's face was priceless. He didn't stare off even once. From that moment on I had him. He read the entire chapter assigned for the day and even tried to read ahead. When we went over the vocabulary words, Shan would tell the rest of the group the definition. Not only did Shan start to feel successful with himself, he also became a critical part of our guiding reading group.

(Andrea Hernandez, New York teacher)

In addition to devices, instructional technologies include video recordings, instructional websites, databases, virtual museums, electronic tutorials, simulations, educational games, broadcast and streaming media, e-books, and other forms of content designed to facilitate learning though individual activities or through creative social engagement with other children and adults. Graphs, charts, symbols, and pictures with captions in multiple languages are good resources that can be used to scaffold instruction. Even though SMART Board communities are a viable option for acquiring content, much more common is the use of the Internet, which provides teachers with opportunities to access and integrate electronic resources into their teaching practices. Such use of the Internet is strongly recommended to enhance instruction in bilingual classrooms. To learn more about the availability of instructional methods and resources, teachers may partner with instructional technology facilitators for professional development and to get tips for integrating technology into teaching practice. Technology facilitators may recommend to teachers particular devices and software useful to students for acquiring literacy skills and content knowledge.

Use of instructional technologies creates an atmosphere in which students interact with media, which many students feel comfortable doing in order to learn and to express themselves. Technologies that respond to user input are said to be *interactive media,* which generally refers to digital devices and application software, commonly called *apps* (National Association for the Education of Young Children, 2012). These interactive technological tools help students attain curricular goals and increase their understanding of the modern technology around them, which they will use frequently. Technological devices and software help students develop cognitive and linguistic skills through unique exercises that challenge students in a visual and auditory way, which increases their vocabulary and proficiency in two languages. Teachers often find it easy to integrate the resources into their lessons because the materials have been tested in actual classrooms and found to be effective for helping students acquire particular curricular objectives. Teachers need to guide students as they acquire digital content and use technology tools to synthesize what they are learning. Use of technologies that capture audio and video can motivate learners and create opportunities for effective learning because of their practicality, straightforward use, low cost, and suitability to particular instructional objectives. As a capstone project to a unit, teachers may require that students synthesize what they have learned and make a presentation to the class using different types of software. Such tasks permit students to express themselves creatively. Supplementing content lessons with instruction on visual design principles before students create their presentations often improves the quality of such production work considerably. Green, Facer, Rudd, Dillon, and Humphreys (2005, p. 3) identified the following features as important to the integration of technology for each learner: (1) Grant learners opportunities to make informed educational decisions; (2) recognize diverse forms of knowledge; (3) create diverse learning environments; and (4) provide learner-focused feedback and assessments. Figure 8.1 lists the guiding principles for the appropriate use of technology for children as published by the National Association for the Education of Young Children (2012).

Figure 8.1. National Association for the Education of Young Children Technology Guiding Principles

- Appropriate use of technology and media depends on the age, developmental level, needs, interests, linguistic background, and abilities of each child.
- Effective uses of technology and media are active, hands-on, engaging, and empowering; give the child control; provide adaptive scaffolds to ease the accomplishment of task; and are used as one of many options to support children's learning.
- When used appropriately, technology and media can enhance children's cognitive and social abilities.
- Interactions with technology and media should be playful and support creativity, exploration, pretend play, active play, and outdoor activities.
- Technology tools can help educators make and strengthen home-school connections.
- Technology and media can enhance early childhood practice when integrated into the environment, curriculum, and daily routines.
- Assistive technology must be available as needed to provide equitable access for children with special needs.
- Technology tools can be effective for dual-language learners by providing access to a family's home language and culture while supporting English language learners.
- Digital literacy is essential to guiding early childhood educators and parents in the selection, use, integration, and evaluation of technology and interactive media.

Source: Excepted from NAEYC, 2012. Full text of this position statement is available at www.naeyc.org/files.naeyc/PS_technology_WEB.pdf.

Organizations such as the National Council of Teachers of Mathematics (NCTM, 2000) have recognized the importance of technology in the teaching/learning process. For example, NCTM includes a "technology principle" as one of six principles of high-quality mathematics education. The principle reads: "Technology is essential in teaching and learning mathematics; it influences the mathematics that is taught and enhances students' learning" (p. 24). In addition, the International Society for Technology in Education (ISTE) has created National Educational Technology Standards for Students (NETS-S), which include (1) creativity and innovation; (2) communication and collaboration; (3) research and information fluency; (4) critical thinking, problem-solving, and decisionmaking; (5) digital citizenship; and (6) technology operations and concepts. Addressing all NETS-S in schools enhances the quality and appropriateness of technological tools to students, especially when challenged to use technologies for content acquisition in two languages. Consistent with NETS-S, bilingual learners ought to be able to identify problems, plan, and conduct analyses and syntheses using appropriate technology tools and resources. By helping young bilingual learners develop their creativity, technology skills, content knowledge, and dual-language competencies, teachers are preparing youth to make significant contributions in our global village.

Schools benefit from research and best practices in technology integration (Lee & Hollebrands, 2008). Technology integration in schools should include (1) access to digital devices; (2) accessible/assistive technologies; (3) distance education; (4) emerging technologies; (5) Internet safety; (6) leadership and technology; (7) teacher practice and professional development; and (8) visual media. Integrating all of these components is important to successful technology integration in schools.

INTEGRATING TECHNOLOGY INTO INSTRUCTION

Educators are challenged to use technology in their teaching in order to expand students' knowledge and skills. Back in the 1980s, Shulman (1981) encouraged teachers to draw on pedagogical and content (subject matter) knowledge to create effective instruction. Extending that notion to include technological knowledge, Mishra and Koehler (2006) encouraged teachers to draw on technological, pedagogical, and content knowledge in order to create effective instruction. Sometimes, just knowing about the availability of a video recording and how students access it on a computer are sufficient for beginning a lesson. Teachers need not be technology experts to begin integrating technology into instruction.

We recommend that teachers use digital videos in the native language as one resource for instruction to help them acquire knowledge and information in the content areas. Over time, after a teacher has learned about video recording (which can be as simple as a couple of finger taps on a smartphone) and video editing, then the teacher may assign students the task of creating a video to synthesize information and demonstrate what they have learned. This activity enables learners to create their own digital videos, learn from the process, and share them with peers. Video production could also involve multiple planning steps, including storyboarding, but those steps need not be undertaken for initial attempts to use this strategy. The planning steps are important for higher-quality video work, but students who create videos to synthesize content knowledge need not obsess about production values. The primary benefit of video production to students is the process of determining what messages to convey, which requires reflection on content and knowledge of the target audience.

Bilingual classroom teachers should consider technology resources that enhance real-world relevance and exploration. Interactive technology, multimedia, and computer activities encourage and motivate students to create and participate in the language development process. Many interactive technologies can be integrated to create a platform for student learning. Educators have multiple tools for including and increasing technology use in the classroom in their quest to design, develop, and utilize instructional activities that will engage students in active and productive learning. When used appropriately in the native language classroom, technologies provide opportunities for bilingual students to apply their background knowledge and take it to a higher level. When bilingual students draw on their native language and find the instructional goal relevant, they will consider the instruction valuable and genuine. Ultimately, genuine learning experiences become evident in the way students apply what they learned in their lives. Technologies can be used as a resource to create such valuable learning experiences. As technology advances, educators need to innovate and find new ways to help learners connect curricular goals encountered in school to applicability in modern society. That takes practice. Such practice is necessary for teachers in the native language classroom to help their students use technology to improve their vocabulary and writing, and to refine their understanding of concepts as they build content knowledge.

Writing Development

Seifoori, Mozaheb, and Beigi (2012) acknowledge that teaching writing is a complex and challenging process and that writing is critically important. In particular, they noted that "writing is one of the most important aspects of language teaching" (p. 107). How can technology help with writing instruction? To begin, technology helps bilingual learners edit, write, spell check, and rewrite their assignments. Some word processing software also displays grammatical errors and bilingual learners are free to reflect on errors and spend the time necessary for them to make changes in attempts to correct the errors. Standard word processing software, with spell check and grammar check capability, provides some assistance to bilingual students as they compose sentences, paragraphs, reports, and essays, for instance. On any occasion when students reflect on their writing and correct their spelling and grammatical errors, they increase their language skills. A nice bonus for bilingual students is that such reflection fosters both native and second language acquisition.

Since there are many purposes for writing, we can encourage writing through text messaging or instant messaging, email, and Facebook notes, for instance. In bilingual classrooms, the teacher and students can share their writing and generate ideas on how to improve their writing skills in the two languages. In addition, the class can engage in an interactive writing activity in an online discussion forum that the teacher closely monitors and guides. It is also possible to assign groups of students to collaborative writing tasks in a wiki. After such writing tasks, the teacher could allow time for independent writing, which would create an opportunity to assess progress. Through a combination of modeling, providing feedback about each student's writing, and accommodations to adjust to different writing levels, teachers play a key role in teaching writing.

Consistent with Vygotsky's (2005) theory of understanding, the use of instructional technologies should be appropriate to the learner's developmental level. As such, teachers need to evaluate websites, instructional videos, and other technological resources before use, as in the following instructional scenario. In a social studies class, taught in Spanish, the teacher gives bilingual learners a writing assignment on a particular contemporary theme (e.g., global warming/*calentamiento global*). After an initial brainstorming session with the students to bring multiple perspectives to the issue, the teacher directs them to a specific webpage, which the teacher has prepared. The webpage contains hyperlinks to webpages of content suitable for students across a range of developmental levels. Some of the content is in the native language of the students; the other webpages are in English. Further, the teacher has been creative in preparing writing assignments appropriate to multiple developmental levels. Each student is required to write a short summary based on his or her writing skill level, and students are allowed to answer in either Spanish or English. These questions are listed in order of increasing complexity, and the teacher would assign one of the questions to each student.

1. ¿Cúal es el mensaje del autor? ¿Qué detalles usa el autor para expresar su idea principal?
   (What is the author's message? What details does the author use to express his or her main ideas?)
2. ¿Cúales son los puntos que se repiten sobre el calentamiento global?
   (Which are the repetitive points on the topic of global warming?)
3. ¿Cómo el autor usa el lenguaje para expresar sus puntos de vista?
   (How does the author use the language to express his or her points of view?)
4. ¿Desde su/tu punto de vista, ¿cúal es su/tu opinión sobre el calentamiento global?
   (From your own perspective, what is your opinion on global warming?)

When teaching writing through the use of technology, proceed one step at a time in order to build the student's confidence. Additionally, educators have to assess and monitor the students' progress and writing success. As Seifoori et al. (2012) stated, "a good teacher should be able to consider the needs of the students, and then decide on the right approach to be used in class" (p. 113). Hofer and Swan (2006) stated, "The knowledge and experience required to integrate technology into teaching and learning is a complex, multi-faceted challenge" (p. 82). Indeed, it is a challenge, but over time, teachers become more adept at using technologies to engage students in effective instructional activities.

Concept Development

Bilingual learners have to understand and comprehend concepts to learn academic content and languages, especially the enhancement of their native one (Mutlu, 2009). Mutlu researched computer-based concept mapping as an effective tool for teaching social studies to bilingual students. She ascertained that computer programs for building graphic organizers promotes social studies content knowledge acquisition. Using concept mapping software, students take ownership of their learning and practice the use of two languages in the classroom. Indeed, a bilingual learner can build conceptual connections in two languages using concept mapping software. The use of two languages increases vocabulary, which better prepares students for academic language across subject areas. Computer-based concept mapping is an excellent technology tool for developing and organizing ideas before reading the books and print materials. The software enables refinements to understanding through visualization, modeling, and multiple representations. The sample concept map in Figure 8.2 demonstrates how to use mapping to make explicit connections between concepts.

Novak and Gowin (1996) discovered that including words between the concepts to make relationships explicit is beneficial for learning. In addition to electronic concept mapping, teachers can use electronic diagrams, planning designs, images, and other graphic organizers creatively in order to increase content understanding.

Vocabulary Development

The building of vocabulary using electronic games is an engaging strategy for improving the linguistic skills in the native and second language. Teachers can use computers to locate or create visual representations of words in the classroom for instruction in both languages. Using images helps students connect the native language with the second language and to make sense of the meanings of words, which may be context dependent. Interactive multimedia resources are powerful tools for helping bilingual learners acquire knowledge and skills. Finally, we suggest that teachers take advantage of digital vocabulary field trips to enhance content knowledge. All of these examples provide ideas for engaging the bilingual learner in school and beyond.

Figure 8.2. A Sample Concept Map

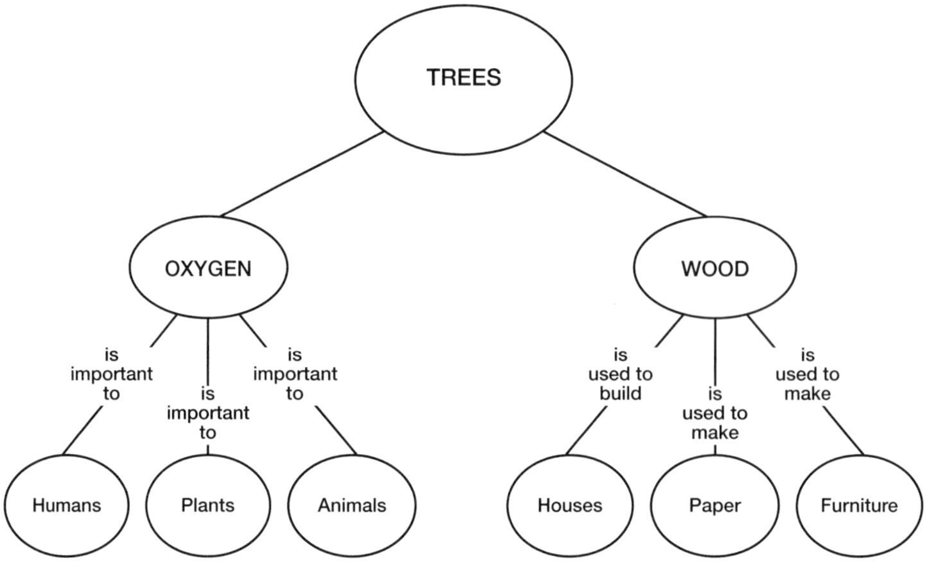

Developed by K. Luterbach, East Carolina University.

Development of Reading Comprehension

Reading comprehension can be enhanced through the use of technology. Essentially, bilingual learners need to use their background knowledge in order to develop sufficient skill to recognize and decode words, build vocabulary in two languages, develop word fluency, increase language processing and understanding, and develop meta-cognition strategies. Teachers may integrate technology into instruction in multiple ways to help bilingual students attain those goals. Through digital storytelling, students create multimedia presentations using narration and photos. Bilingual learners can create music videos, short stories, *novelas* (soap operas), and biographies; identify important events in their personal lives; or describe a country's history, for instance. Teachers need to create tasks that are developmentally appropriate for their students and aligned with curricular standards. Using multiple forms of expression, bilingual learners enjoy sharing information with their peers. A person with command of two or more languages can share information with more people than a monolingual person. Outside the United States, personal use of two languages is very common. In our globally connected world, technologies mediate communication. In schools, virtual classroom connections between one country and another enable the exchange of information between students with diverse backgrounds. Global networking uses technology to connect groups of people around the world, which enables exchanges of information in two languages. Such interactive global exchanges in classrooms are meaningful and useful for practicing reading, writing, listening, and speaking in two languages. Another use of technology for learning involves requiring or encouraging students to create a story map, which is a visual depiction of the elements of a short story. Story maps can be implemented in two languages, as shown in Figure 8.3.

Figure 8.3. Sample Story Maps in English and Hindi

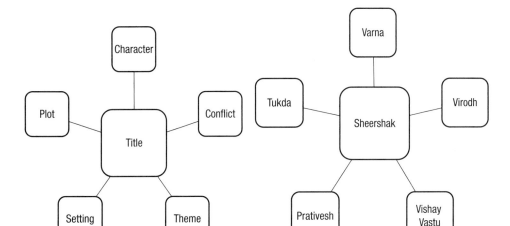

Development of Content Area Knowledge

Technology is useful for the development of content knowledge, including, for instance, facts, concepts, processes, principles, and strategies. Technologies help bilingual learners connect ideas and identify relevant information, as well as sort and prioritize information. To help students identify relevant information about various places, students may use the World Wide Web to go on virtual tours. Virtual touring is one way to diminish the "confines" of your classroom. For example, students can make virtual visits to the museums in their native countries using the web or teachers may choose to guide the tour initially and then permit individual exploration. This type of activity promotes diversity and engages the students in a way that invites learning and fosters respect for their own and other cultures and languages. Prior to the presentation or tour, teachers may develop background knowledge. For example, the teacher may challenge students to assess how much they know about a particular topic.

Electronic tutorials are also a good way of expanding students' content knowledge. In educational settings, the bilingual learner should be taught the necessary skills to be successful in academic settings. We suggest implementing literacy strategies using software. For example, if teachers want students to monitor their reading comprehension and speaking skills, they could have students read text, and then compare themselves to recorded speech or to the sounds produced by speech synthesis software for the same text. To help bilingual learners conceive of concepts or procedures visually, students may be directed to use software for creating graphic organizers. To help bilingual learners answer questions, generate questions, and use text structures, teachers might want to provide students with computer-based writing templates. To help bilingual learners write and express themselves, students may use text editing or word processing software. Text editors may be embedded in applications, such as email client software or stand-alone applications such as Notepad and TextEdit, which are bundled with popular operating systems.

All these electronic tools benefit students' acquisition of language, literacy, and subject area content (Graham, Cagiltay, Lim, Craner, & Duffy, 2001). If well implemented, technology can (1) encourage student-teacher contact and interaction; (2) encourage cooperation among students; (3) encourage active learning; (4) give prompt feedback; (5) emphasize time on task; (6) communicate high expectations; and (7) respect diverse talents and ways of learning. Building trust with bilingual learners and encouraging them to be self-confident and self-regulated in their learning is imperative in the bilingual classroom. Technology is a platform that many bilingual learners can use to practice, learn, experience, and exchange information in academic settings; it encourages bilingual learners to use their linguistic abilities in the native and second language.

WEBSITES AS EDUCATIONAL RESOURCES

Teachers need to learn to integrate technologies into their teaching practices (Herrington, Herrington, & Mantei, 2009; Van den Akker, 1999; Wang & Hannafin, 2005). One way instructional technologists can assist teachers is by maintaining lists of the diverse educational websites, which address a variety of topics and needs. Some websites contain tutorials for instruction in specific content areas, while other websites store raw data, such as the spreadsheets and databases at state education agencies. Professional organizations often include instructional resources in their websites. Certain government agencies also maintain websites of educational resources. For example, more than 1,600 teaching and learning resources, organized by subject (art, health and physical education, history, language arts, math, science, and world studies), are accessible at the Federal Resources for Educational Excellence website. Websites of some philanthropic foundations and nonprofit organizations also include content for teachers. For example, the Colorín Colorado website contains information and resources appropriate for dual-language classrooms. Collectively, they provide resources for all subject areas. We encourage teachers and parents to consider the native language of bilingual learners and to search for appropriate resources and websites in the native language.

We also recommend that teachers go to websites of different countries' consulates for additional, and perhaps more language-appropriate, information. Also, by searching for instructional resources on websites of school districts around the world, teachers may find information that can be used with few modifications in their native language classrooms.

Afterword

I read this book manuscript while doing Fulbright work in Macau, a region with a fast-growing economy and $60,000 per capita income. The government here provides free medical care to all its residents and free preschool education to all young children. People here speak many languages (e.g., English, Portuguese, Mandarin, Cantonese, etc.), and do business with countries in Europe, South America, North America, and Asia. Public and private schools use English, Portuguese, and Chinese for instruction, and the students have access to many opportunities without getting confused and losing their native languages.

The Bilingual Advantage offers an integration of theories, research, and practices that can greatly benefit researchers, educators, advocates, and family members. It is a resource that is published at the right time, as we prepare our students for the 21st century, to be globally competitive, and to help the United States to retain its leading edge in the world. It is important that we move beyond policies that have discouraged the development of bilingual and biliterate students, and join with emerging economies and countries with fast-growing economies that encourage and support students and citizens to become globally competent.

This book offers rationale and evidence that include research findings about the advantages of being bilingual and biliterate. Armed with such information, we need to use our collective wisdom and research evidence in starting conversations and collaboration about how to make this happen.

Practically, this book offers many examples, models, and strategies for supporting our students to become bilingual and biliterate. The strategies and examples provide clear road maps for how to make this a reality for our students. This book also introduces a comprehensive perspective in examining how native language instruction can be used in different models (e.g., ESL, dual-language model, inclusive special education classes, etc.). The practical and useful ideas and strategies can be seen in tools for instruction, assessment, resources for teachers and parents, and reflection throughout this book.

We, as educators and researchers, can use this resource to think, plan, and educate our students in ways that help them to retain this valuable asset, that is, being bilingual and biliterate, so that they will be better connected to their own families, their communities, and people of other countries; have access to expanded opportunities for learning and employment; bring this asset to contribute to our position in a world economy; and more important, navigate, live, and work freely in this global environment.

Chun Zhang

References

Alanis, I., & Rodríguez, M. (2008). Sustaining a dual language immersion program: Features of success. *Journal of Latinos & Education, 7,* 305–319.

Amaral, O., Garrison, L., & Klentschy, M. (2002). Helping English learners increase achievement through inquiry-based science instruction. *Bilingual Research Journal, 26*(2), 213–239.

Americans with Disabilities Act of 1990 (ADA), 42 U.S.C. §§ 12101-12213.

Amour, M. (2003). Connecting children's stories to children's literature: Meeting diversity needs. *Early Childhood Education, 31*(1), 47–51.

Anderson, L., & Krathwohl, D. (2000) *A taxonomy for learning, teaching, and assessing: A revision of Bloom's taxonomy of educational objectives.* Boston, MA: Allyn & Bacon.

Aquirre-Muñoz, Z. (2010). *Teaching math to diverse adolescent leaners: Instructional equity guide.* Texas Tech University, TX: West Texas Middle School Math Science Partnership.

Artiles, A. J., Kozleski, E. B., & Waitoller, F. (2011). *Inclusive education: Examining equity of five continents.* Cambridge, MA: Harvard Education Press.

Artiles, A. J., & Ortiz, A. (Eds.). (2002). *English language learners with special needs: Identification, assessment, instruction.* Washington, DC: The Center for Applied Linguistics.

Aspira of New York. (1974, August 29). Decision accompanying the Consent Decree. 72 Civ. 4002 S.D.Y.

Association of Latino Administrators & Superintendents. (2011). *Using technology to prepare ELLs in math for college and career.* Marlborough, MA: ALEKS Corporation and the Association of Latino Administrators & Superintendents.

Auerbach, E. (1993). Reexamining English only in the ESL classroom. *TESOL Quarterly, 27*(1), 19.

August, D., Artzi, L., & Mazrum, J. (2010). Improving science and vocabulary learning of English language learners. Retrieved from www.cal.org/create/resources/pubs/pdfs/create-brief-academic-language.pdf

August, D., Carlo, M., Dressler, C., & Snow, C. (2005). The critical role of vocabulary development for English language learners. *Learning Disabilities Research and Practice, 20*(1), 50–57.

August, D., & Shanahan, T. (Eds.). (2006a). *Developing literacy in the second language learners: A report of national panel on language-minority children and youth.* Mahwah, NJ: Lawrence Erlbaum Associates.

August, D., & Shanahan, T. (Eds.). (2006b). *Developing reading and writing in second language learners: Lessons from the Report of the National Literacy Panel on language-minority children and youth.* New York: Routledge.

Baca, L. M., & Cervantes, H. T. (2004). *The bilingual special education interface* (4th edition). Upper Saddle River, NJ: Pearson.

Baker, C. (2006). *Foundations of bilingual education and bilingualism.* Clevedon, UK: Multilingual Matters.

Balderrama, M., & Diaz-Rico, L. (2006). *Teaching performance expectations for educating English learners.* Boston, MA: Pearson.

Bermúdez, A. B., & Márquez, J. A. (1996). An examination of a four-way collaborative to increase parental involvement in the schools. *Journal of Educational Issues of Language Minority Students, 16,* 1–16.

Bhatt, S. (1988). *Brunizem.* Manchester, UK: Carcanet Press

Bialystok, E. (1987a). Influences of bilingualism on metalinguistic development. *Second Language Research, 3*(2), 154–166.

Bialystok, E. (1987b). Words as things: Development of word concept by bilingual children. *Studies in Second Language Learning, 9,* 133–140.

Bialystok E. (1988). Levels of bilingualism and levels of linguistic awareness. *Developmental Psychology, 24,* 560–567.

Bialystok, E. (1997). Effects of bilingualism and billiteracy on children's emerging concepts of print. *Developmental Psychology, 33*(3) 429–440.

Bialystok, E. (1999). Cognitive complexity and attentional control in the bilingual mind. *Child Development, 70,* 636–644.

Bialystok, E. (2001). *Bilingualism in development: Language, literacy, and cognition.* New York: Cambridge University Press.

Bialystok, E., Barac, R., Blaye, A., & Poulin-Dubois, D. (2010): Word mapping and executive functioning in young monolingual and bilingual children. *Journal of Cognition and Development, 11*(4), 485–508.

Bialystok, E., & Craik, F. I. M. (2010). Cognitive and linguistic processing in the bilingual mind. *Current Directions in Psychological Science, 19,* 19–23.

Bialystok, E., Craik, F. I. M., Klein, R., & Wiswanathan, M. (2004). Bilingualism, aging, and cognitive control: Evidence from the Simon task. *Psychology and Aging, 19,* 290–303.

Bialystok, E., & Hakuta, K. (1994). *In other words: The science and psychology of second language acquisition.* New York: Basic Books.

Bialystok, E., Luk, G., & Kwan, E. (2005). Bilingualism, biliteracy, and learning to read: Interaction among languages and writing systems, *Scientific Studies of Reading, 9*(1), 43–61.

Bialystok, E., Luk, G., Peets, K. F., & Yang, S. (2010). Receptive vocabulary: Differences in monolingual and bilingual children. *Bilingualism: Language and Cognition, 13(4)* 525–531.

Bialystok, E., & Martin, M. (2004). Attention and inhibition in bilingual children: Evidence from the dimensional change card sort task. *Developmental Science, 7*(3), 325–339.

Bilingual Education Act (1968). Public Law 95-561.

Bloom, B. (1956). *Taxonomy of educational objectives: The classification of educational goals, by a committee of college and university examiners.* New York: Longmans.

Bloomfield, L. (1933). *Language.* New York: Holt.

Bowman-Perrott, L. J., Herrera, S., & Murry, K. (2010). Reading difficulties and grade retention: What's the connection for English language learners? *Reading & Writing Quarterly, 26,* 91–107.

Brice, A., & Roseberry-McKibbin, C. (2001). Choice of language in instruction: One language or two? *Teaching exceptional children, 33*(4), 10–16.

Brown, B., & Ryoo, K. (2008). Teaching science as a language: A "content-first" approach to science teaching. *Journal of Research in Science Teaching, 45*(5), 529–553.

Calderón, M. (2007). *Teaching reading to English language learners, grades 6–12: A framework for improving achievement in the content areas.* Thousand Oaks, CA: Corwin Press.

Calderón, M., & Minaya-Rowe, L. (2003). *Designing and implementing two-way bilingual programs.* Thousand Oaks, CA: Corwin Press.

California Department of Education. (1992). *Handbook for teaching Korean-American students.* Sacramento, CA: Author.

California Department of Education. (2011). *California English language development test (CELDT): 2011-12 CELDT information guide.* Retrieved from www.cde.ca.gov/ta/tg/el/documents/celdtinfoguide1112.pdf

Calkins, L. (1994). *The art of teaching writing.* Portsmouth, NH: Heinemann.

Cardenas, J. A. (1986). The role of native language instruction in bilingual education. *Phi Delta Kappan International, 67*(5) 359–363.

Carlson, S. M., & Meltzoff, A. N. (2008). Bilingual experience and executive functioning in young children. *Developmental Science, 11,* 279–295.

Carrasquillo, A. (1993). Whole native language instruction for limited-English-proficient students. In A. Carrasquillo & C. Hedley (Eds.), *Whole language and the bilingual learner* (pp. 3–19). Norwood, NJ: Ablex Publishing.

Carrasquillo, A. (1994). *Teaching English as a second language: A resource guide.* New York: Garland.

Carrasquillo, A. (2010). *Perceived benefits of bilingualism.* Paper presented at the New York State Association for Bilingual Education, New York.

Carrasquillo, A. (2011). *A closer look at dual language instruction at PS/MS 218: K–2.* New York: Bilingual / ESL Technical Assistance Center (BETAC). Unpublished manuscript.

Carrasquillo, A., & Buttaro, L. (2006). *Easy steps for implementing and evaluating a dual language program.* New York: Linus.

Carrasquillo, A., Kucer, S., & Abrams, R. (2004). *Beyond the beginnings.* New York: Multilingual Matters.

Carrasquillo, A., & London, C. (1993) *Parents and schools*: New York: Garland.

Carrasquillo, A., & Rodríguez, V. (2002). *Language minority students in the mainstream classroom* (2nd ed.). New York: Multilingual Matters.

Carrasquillo, A., & Segan, P. (Eds.). (1998). *The teaching of reading to the bilingual student/La enseñanza de lectura para el estudiante bilingue.* Mahwah, NJ: Lawrence Erlbaum Associates.

Carreira, M. (2007). Spanish-for-native speaker matters: Narrowing the Latino achievement gap through Spanish language instruction. *Heritage Language Journal, 5*(1), 147–172.

Center for Applied Linguistics. (2012). Directory of two-way bilingual immersion programs in the U.S. Retrieved from www.cal.org/twi/directory/

Chapelle, C. A. (2003) *English language learning and technology.* Amsterdam, Netherlands: John Benjamin.

Christian, D. (1994). *Two-way bilingual education: Students learning through two languages.* Washington, DC: National Center for Research on Cultural Diversity and Second Language Learning.

Christian, D. (2011). Dual language education. In Hinkel, E. (Ed.), *Handbook of research in second language teaching and learning.* Vol. 2 (pp. 3–20). New York: Routledge.

Chu, H. (1993). *The Korean Americans, multiethnic reminder.* (ED371106).

Cloud, N., Genesee, F., & Hamayan, E. (2000). *Dual language instruction: A handbook of enriched education.* Boston, MA: Heinle & Heinle.

Cobb, B., Vega, D., & Kronauge, C. (2009). Effect of elementary dual language immersion school program on junior high school achievement. In D. L. Hough, *Middle grades research: Exemplary studies linking theory and practice* (pp. 1–20). Charlotte, NC: Information Age.

Collier, V. (1987). Age and rate of acquisition of second language for academic purposes. *TESOL Quarterly, 23*(2), 509–532.

Collier, V. (1992). The Canadian bilingual immersion debate: A synthesis of research findings. *Studies in Second Language Acquisition, 14*(1), 87–97.

Collier, V., & Thomas, W. (1989). How quickly can immigrants become proficient in school English? *Journal of Educational Issues of Language Minority Students, 5*, 26–38.

Collier, V., & Thomas, W. (2004). The astounding effectiveness of dual language education for all. *NABE Journal of Research and Practice, 2*, 1–20.

Conboy, B. T., & Mills, D. L. (2006). Two languages, one developing brain: Event-related potentials to words in bilingual toddlers. *Developmental Science, 9*(1), F1–F12.

Crawford, J. (2004). *Educating English learners: Language diversity in the classroom*: Los Angeles, CA: Bilingual Education Services.

Cromdal, J. (1999). Childhood bilingualism and metalinguistic skills: Analysis and control in young Swedish-English bilinguals. *Applied Psycholinguistics, 20*, 1–20.

Cummins, J. (1979a). Cognitive/academic language proficiency, linguistic interdependence, the optimum age question. *Working Papers on Bilingualism, 19*, 121–129.

Cummins, J. (1979b). Linguistic interdependence and the educational development of bilingual children. *Review of Educational Research, 49*, 222–251.

Cummins, J. (1981). The role of primary language development in promoting educational success for language minority students. In D. P. Dolton (Ed.), *Schooling and language minority students: A theoretical framework* (pp. 3–49). Los Angeles, CA: Evaluation, Dissertation, and Assessment Center.

Cummins, J. (1984). *Bilingual education and special education: Issues in assessment and pedagogy*. San Diego, CA: College Hill.

Cummins, J. (1989). *Empowering minority students*. Sacramento, CA: California Association for Bilingual Education.

Cummins, J. (1991). Independence of first-second-language proficiency in bilingual children. In E. Bialystok (Ed.), *Language processing in bilingual children* (pp. 70-89). Cambridge, UK: Cambridge University Press.

Cummins, J. (2000). *Language, power and pedagogy: Bilingual children in the crossfire*. Buffalo, NY: Multilingual Matters.

Cummins, J. (2005). Language proficiency, bilingualism, and academic achievement. In P. Richard-Amato & M. Snow (Ed.), *Academic success for English language learners: Strategies for K-12 mainstream teachers* (pp. 76–86). White Plains, NY: Pearson Education.

Cummins, J. (2011). *Putting the evidence back into evidenced-based policies for underachieving students*. Strasbourg: Council of Europe.

Cummins, J., & Mulcahy, R. (1978). Orientation to language in Ukrainian-English bilingual children. *Child Development, 49*, 1239–1242.

Cummins, J., and Swain, M. (1986). *Bilingualism in education: Aspects of theory, research, and practice*. London: Longman.

Darcy, N. T. (1946). The effects of bilingualism upon the measurement of the intelligence of children of preschool age. *The Journal of Educational Psychology, 37*, 21–44.

Darcy, N. T. (1963). Bilingualism and the measure of intelligence: Review of a decade of research. *Journal of Genetic Psychology, 103*, 259–282.

Dehaene-Lambertz, G., Hertz-Pannier, L., Dubois, J., & Dehaene, S. (2008). How does brain organization promote language acquisition in humans? *European Review, 16*, 399–411.

Demmert, W. J., & Towner, J. C. (2003). *A review of the research literature on the influences of culturally based education on the academic performance of Native American Students*. Portland, OR: Northwest Regional Educational Laboratory

Diamond, A. (2002). Normal development of prefrontal cortex from birth to young adulthood: Cognitive functions, anatomy and biochemistry. In D. T. Stuss & R. Knight (Eds.), *Principles of frontal lobe function* (pp. 466–503). New York: Oxford.

Diaz, R. M. (1985). Bilingual cognitive development: Addressing three gaps in current research. *Child Development, 56*, 1376–1388.

Diaz-Rico, L. (2004). *Teaching English learners: Strategies and methods*. Boston, MA: Pearson.

Diaz-Rico, L. (2008). *Strategies for teaching English learners* (2nd ed.). Boston, MA: Allyn & Bacon.

Douglas, R., Klentschy, M., Worth, K., & Binder, W. (Eds.). (2006). *Linking science and literacy in the K–8 classroom*. Arlington, VA: National Science Teacher Association.

Duguay, A. (2012). A comprehensive model for instruction of academic language and literacy in the content areas. Retrieved from www.cal.org/create/resources/pubs/pdfs/comprehensive-model-for-instruction-of-academic-language-literacy-in-the-content-areas.pdf

Duke, N., & Pearson, P. (2002). Effective practices for developing reading comprehension. In A. E. Farstrup & J. Samuels (Eds.), *What research has to say about reading instruction* (3rd ed., pp. 205–242). Newark, NJ: Delaware: International Reading Association.

Dunkel, P. (1986). Developing listening fluency in L2: Theoretical principles and pedagogical considerations. *Modern Language Journal, 70*(2), 99–106.

Echevarria, J., & Graves, A. (2011). *Sheltered content instruction: Teaching English language learners with diverse abilities* (4th ed.). Boston, MA: Pearson Education Inc.

Echevarria, J., Vogt, M., & Short, D. (2010). *Making content comprehensible for secondary English learners: The SIOP model*. Boston, MA: Allyn & Bacon.

Estrada, V. L., Gómez, L., & Ruiz-Escalante, J. A. (2009). Let's make dual language the norm. *Educational Leadership, 66*(7), 54–58.

Fang-Ying, Y. (2009). *Biliteracy effects of phonological awareness, oral language proficiency, and reading skills in Taiwanese Mandarin-English bilingual children* (Dissertations and theses from the University of Illinois at Urbana-Champaign). Retrieved from www.ideals.illinois.edu/handle/2142/14709

Florida State Department of Education. (n.d.). *District plan for English language learners (ELLs)*. Retrieved from www.fldoe.org/aala/ELLPlans/2009/Pky09.pdf

Florida State Department of Education. (2011). *Requirements for identification, eligibility, and programmatic assessments of English language learners*. Retrieved from www.flrules.org/gateway/ruleNo.asp?id=6A-6.0902

Fradd, S., Lee, O., Sutman, F., & Saxton, M. (2002). Materials development promoting science inquiry with English language learners: A case study. *Bilingual Research Journal, 25*, 479–501.

Freeman, D. E., & Freeman, Y. S. (2004). *Essential linguistics: What you need to know to teach reading, ESL, spelling, phonics, and grammar*. Portsmouth, NH: Heinemann.

Freeman, Y. S., & Freeman, D. E. (2008a). *Academic language for English language learners and struggling readers*. Portsmouth, NH: Heinemann.

Freeman, Y. S., & Freeman, D. E. (2008b). English language learners: Who are they? How can teachers support them? In Y. Freeman, D. Freeman, & R. Ramirez (Eds.), *Diverse learners in the mainstream classroom* (pp. 31–59). Portsmouth, NH: Heinemann.

Freeman, Y. S., Freeman, D. E., & Mercuri, S. P. (2005). *Dual language essentials for teachers and administrators*. Portsmouth, NH: Heinemann.

Galambos, S. J., & Goldin-Meadow, S. (1990). The effects of learning two languages on level of metalinguistic awareness. *Cognition, 34,* 1–56.

Galambos, S. J., & Hakuta, K. (1988). Subject-specific and task-specific characteristics of meta-linguistic awareness in bilingual children. *Applied Psycholinguistics, 9,* 141–162.

García, E. (2005). *Teaching and learning in two languages.* New York: Teachers College Press.

Gardner, H. (1983). *Framed of mind.* New York: Knopf.

Gardner, H. (2006) *Changing minds: The art and science of changing our own and other people's minds.* Boston, MA: Harvard Business School Press.

Genesee, F. (1989). Early bilingual development: One language or two? *Journal of Child Language, 16,* 161–179.

Genesee, F., Lindholm-Leary, K., Saunders, W., & Christian, D. (2006). *Educating English language learners: A synthesis of research evidence.* Cambridge, UK: Cambridge University Press.

Goals 2000: Educate America Act. Public Law 103-227.

Goetz, P. J. (2003). The effects of bilingualism on theory of mind development. *Bilingualism: Language and Cognition, 6,* 1–15.

Goldenberg, C. (2006). Improving achievement for English learners. *Education Week,* 13–14. Retrieved from www.edweek.org/ew/articles/2006/07/26/43goldenberg.h25.html?qs=july,+2006

Goldenberg, C. (2008). Teaching English language learners: What the research does—and does not—say. *American Educator, 32,* 8–23, 42–44. Retrieved from archive.aft.org/pubsreports/american_educator/issues/summer08/goldenberg.pdf

Gomez, L., Freeman, D., & Freeman, Y. (2005). Dual language education: A promising 50-50 model. *Bilingual Research Journal, 29,* 145–164.

Graham, C., Cagiltay, K., Lim, B. R., Craner, J., & Duffy, T. (2001). Seven principles of effective teaching: A practical lens for evaluating online courses. The technology source archives at the University of North Carolina. Retrieved from technologysource.org/article/seven_principles_of_effective_teaching/

Graham, S., & Perin, D. (2007). *Writing next: Effective strategies to improve writing of adolescents in middle and high schools.* Washington, DC: Alliance for Excellence Education

Grant, M., & Lapp, D. (2011). Teaching science literacy. *Educational Leadership, 68*(6). Retrieved from www.ascd.org/publications/educational-leadership/mar11/vol68/num06/Teaching-Science-Literacy.aspx

Green, H., Facer, K., Rudd, T., Dillon, P., & Humphreys, P. (2005). *Personalization and digital technologies.* Bristol: Futurelab. Retrieved from www.futurelab.org.uk/resources/documents/opening_education/Personalisation_report.pdf

Haagar, D., & Klingner, J. (2005) *Differentiating Instruction in Inclusive settings.* Boston, MA: Pearson.

Hadi-Tabassum, S. (2005). The balancing act of bilingual immersion. *Educational Leadership, 62*(4), 50–54.

Hakuta, K. (1986). *Mirror of language: The debate on bilingualism.* New York: Basic Books.

Hamayan, E. V., & Damico, J. S. (1991). *Limiting bias in the assessment of bilingual students.* Austin, TX: Pro-ed.

Hernandez-Sheets, R. (2005). *Diversity pedagogy: Examining the role of culture in the teaching-learning process.* Boston, MA: Allyn & Bacon.

Herrera, S. (2010). *Biography-driven culturally responsive teaching.* New York: Teachers College Press.

Herrera, S., & Murry, K. (2007). *ESL methods module.* Manhattan, KS: Center of Intercultural and Multilingual Advocacy.

Herrington, A., Herrington, J., & Mantei, J. (2009). Design principles for mobile learning. In J. Herrington, A. Herrington, J. Mantei, I. Olney, & B. Ferry (Eds.), *New technologies, new pedagogies: Mobile learning in higher education* (pp. 129–138). Wollongong: University of Wollongong. Retrieved from ro.uow.edu.au/

Hofer, M., & Swan, K. O. (2006). Technological pedagogical content knowledge in action: A case study of a middle school digital documentary project. *Journal of Research on Technology in Education, 41*(2), 179–200.

Hoover, J. H., & Collier, C. (1985). Referring culturally different children: Sociocultural considerations. *Academic Therapy, 20,* 503–509.

Hoover, J., Klingner, Baca, L., & Patton, J. (2008). *Methods for teaching culturally and linguistically diverse exceptional learners.* Boston, MA: Pearson.

Hornberger, N. (2003). *Continua of biliteracy: An ecological framework for educational policy, research, and practice in multilingual settings.* Clevedon, UK: Multilingual Matters.

Improving America's Schools Act of 1994. Public Law 103-382

Individual with Disabilities Education Act of 1990, 20 U.S.C. § 300.1 *et seq.*

Individuals with Disabilities Education Improvement Act, Pub. L., No. 108-446, 118 Stat. 2647 (2004).

Jager, A. (2010). Advancing our students' language and literacy. *American Educator, 53,* 1–11.

Kamil, M. L. (2003). *Adolescents and literacy: Reading for the 21st century.* Washington, DC: Alliance for Excellence in Education.

Karathanos, K. (2009). Exploring US mainstream teachers' perspectives on use of the native language in instruction with English language learner students. *International Journal of Bilingual Education and Bilingualism, 12*(6), 615–633.

Kea, C., Campbell, G. D., & Richards, H. V. (2004). *Becoming culturally responsive educators: Rethinking education pedagogy: Practitioner brief series.* Denver, CO: National Center for Culturally Responsive Educational System.

Kim, K. H. S., Relkin, N., Lee, K. M., & Hirsh, J. (1997). Distinct cortical areas associated with native and second languages. *Nature, 388,* 171–174.

Kirk Senesac, B. V. (2002). Two-way bilingual immersion: A portrait of quality schooling. *Bilingual Research Journal, 26,* 85–102.

Klingner, J. (2004). The science of professional development. *The Journal of Learning Disabilities, 37*(3), 248–255.

Kovelman, I., Baker, S. A., & Petitto, L. A. (2008). Age of first bilingual language exposure as a new window into bilingual reading development. *Bilingualism: Language and Cognition, 11*(2) 203–223.

Kovelman, I., & Petitto, L. A. (2003). *Stages of language development in bilingual children exposed to their other language at different ages.* Poster presented at the annual meeting of the International Symposium on Bilingualism, Phoenix, AZ.

Krashen, S. (1982). *Principles and practice in second language acquisition.* New York: Pergamon Press.

Lake, R. (1990). An Indian Father's Plea. *Teacher Magazine, 2*(1) 48–53.

Lau v. Nichols. 414 US 563 (1974).

Lee, H., & Hollebrands, K. (2008). Preparing to teach mathematics with technology: An integrated approach to developing technological pedagogical content knowledge. *Contemporary Issues in Technology and Teacher Education* [Online serial], *8*(4). Retrieved from www.cite-journal.org/vol8/iss4/mathematics/article1.com

Lee, K. S. (2004). *Cultural / learning and linguistic characteristics of Korean students in the United States: Perceptions of professors and students* (Doctoral dissertation). Fordham University Graduate School of Education, NY.

Lee, K. S. (2010). *Teachers' perceptions on the role of native language instruction.* Paper presented at the New York State Association for Bilingual Education, New York City, March 4–5.

Lee, O., Maerten-Rivera, J., Penfield, R., LeRoy, K., & Secada, W. (2008). Science achievement of English language learners in urban elementary schools: Results of a first year professional development intervention. *Journal of Research in Science Teaching, 45*(1), 31–52.

Lessow-Hurley, J. (2005). *The foundations of dual language instruction* (4th ed.). New York: Addison Wesley Longman.

Lindholm, K. J., & Aclan, Z. (1991). Bilingual proficiency as a bridge to academic achievement: Results from bilingual/immersion programs. *Journal of Education, 173,* 71–80.

Lindholm-Leary, K. J. (2001). *Dual language education.* Tonawanda, NY: Multilingual Matters.

Lindholm-Leary, K. J. (2004/2005). The rich promise of two-way immersion. *Educational Leadership, 62*(4), 56–59.

Lindsay, J. (2010). *Children's access to print material and education-related outcomes: Findings from a meta-analysis review.* Naperville, IL: Learning Point Associates.

Lowman, J. (1990). Promoting motivation and learning. *College Teacher, 38*(4), 136–139.

Lukes, M. (2011). "I understand English but can't write it": The power of native language instruction for adult English learners. *International Multilingual Research Journal, 5,* 19–38.

Luterbach, K. (2013). Elegant instruction. *Journal of Educational Technology Systems, 41*(2) 183–204.

Luterbach, K., Rodriguez, D., & Love, L. (2012). Toward effective and compelling instruction for high school eCommerce students: Results from a small field study. *TechTrends, 56*(6) 59–63.

Lyster, R. (2007). *Learning and teaching languages through content: A counterbalanced approach.* Amsterdam, Netherlands: John Benjamin.

Maltiz, F. (1975). *Living and learning in two languages: Bilingual-bicultural education in United States.* New York: McGraw-Hill.

Mechelli, A., Crinion, J. T., Noppeney, U., O'Doherty, J., Ashburner, J., Frackowiak, R. S., & Price, C. J. (2004). Neurolinguitics: Structural plasticity in the bilingual brain. *Nature, 431*(7010), 757.

Migration Policy Institute. (2010a). *ELL information center fact sheet series.* Retrieved from www.migrationinformation.org/ellinfo/FactSheet_ELL3.pdf

Migration Policy Institute. (2010b). *Number and growth of students in US schools in need of English instruction.* Retrieved from www.migrationinformation.org/ellinfo/FactSheet_ELL1.pdf

Mishra, P., & Koehler, M. J. (2006). Technological pedagogical content knowledge: A framework for teacher knowledge. *Teachers College Record, 108*(6), 1017–1054.

Mohan, B. (1986). *Language and content.* Reading, MA: Addison-Wesley.

Moll, L., Amanti, C., Neff, D., & Gonzalez, N. (1992). Funds of knowledge for teaching: Using a qualitative approach to connect homes and classrooms. *Theory and Practice, 32*(2) 132–141.

Mora, P. (1985). *Chants.* Houston, TX: Arte Público Press.

Mutlu, B. (2009). Computer based concept mapping: An effective academic tool for social studies teachers to help with linguistic and academic development of English language learners. *Social Science Research and Practice, 4*(3), 86–96.

National Association for the Education of Young Children. (2012). *Technology and interactive media as tools in early childhood programs serving children from birth through age 8. Position Statement.* Washington, DC: Author

National Center for Education Statistics. (n.d.) *Fast Facts*. U.S. Department of Education Institute of Education Science. Retrieved from nces.ed.gov/fastfacts/display.asp?id=96

National Council of Teachers of Mathematics. (2000). *Principles and standards for school mathematics*. Reston, VA: Author.

National Government Association Center for Best Practices & Council of Chief State School Officers. (2010a). *Common Core State Standards for English language arts & literacy in history/social studies, science, and technical subjects*. Retrieved from www.corestandards.org/assets/Appendix_A.pdf

National Government Association Center for Best Practices & Council of Chief State School Officers. (2010b). *Application of common core state standards for English language learners*. Retrieved from www.corestandards.org/assets/application-for-english-learners.pdf

National Research Council. (1998). *Preventing reading difficulties in young children*. C. E. Snow, M. S. Burns, and P. Griffin (Eds.). Washington, DC: National Academic Press.

New York City Department of Education. (2011). *The 2010-11 demographics of NY City's English language learners*. Retrieved from schools.nyc.gov/NR/rdonlyres/3A4AEC4C-14BD-49C4-B2E6-8EDF5D873BE4/108227/DemoRpt0722.pdf

New York State Education Department. (2011). *Bilingual education*. Retrieved from www.p12.nysed.gov/biling/bilinged

Nieto, S. (2000). *Affirming diversity: The sociopolitical context of multicultural education* (3rd ed.). New York: Allyn & Bacon.

Nieto, S. (2005). We speak many tongues: Language diversity and multicultural education. In P. Richard-Amato, & M. Snow (Ed.), *Academic success for English language learners: Strategies for K–12 mainstream teachers* (pp. 133–149). White Plains, NY: Pearson Education.

No Child Left Behind Act of 2001. Public Law 107-110.

Novak, J. D., & Gowin, D. B. (1996). *Learning how to learn*. Cambridge, UK: Cambridge University Press.

Nunley, K. F. (2010, June). The advantages of bilingualism. *Layered Curriculum*, 1–2.

Odlin, T. (1989). *Language transfer: Cross-linguistic influence in language learning*. New York: Cambridge University Press.

O'Malley, M. J., & Valdez Pierce, L. (1996). *Authentic assessment for English language learners: Practical approaches for teachers*. New York: Longman.

Ortiz, A. (2001). English language learners with special needs effective instructional strategies. (EDO-FL-01-08).

Ovando, C., & Collier, V. (1998). *Bilingual and ESL classroom: Teaching in multicultural connected thought* (2nd ed.). Boston, MA: McGraw-Hill.

Parchia, C. T. (2000) *Preparing for the future: Experiences and perceptions of African Americans in two-way bilingual immersion programs*. Doctoral dissertation, School of Education, Harvard University.

Parkes, J., & Ruth, T. (2009). *Urgent research questions and issues in dual language education*. Albuquerque, NM: Dual Language Education of New Mexico.

Parson, P., & Rubin, R. (2008). Literacy in a diverse society. In Y. Freeman, D. Freeman, & R. Ramirez (Ed.), *Diverse learners in the mainstream classroom* (pp. 193–210). Portsmouth, NH: Heinemann.

Peregoy, S., & Boyle, O. (2005). *Reading, writing, and learning in ESL: A resource book for K–12 teachers* (4th ed., vol. 3, pp. 100–116). New York: Pearson.

Petitto, L. A. (2009). New discoveries from the bilingual brain and mind across the life span: Implication for education. *International Mind, Brain, and Education Society, 3*(4), 185–197.

Ramírez, J., Yuen, S., & Ramey, D. (1991). *Longitudinal study of structured English immersion strategy, early exit and late exit transitional bilingual programs for language minority children.* Washington, DC: U.S. Department of Education.

Ray, J. M. (2009). A template analysis of teacher agency at an academically successful dual language school. *Journal of Advanced Academics, 21*, 110–141.

Resnick, M. (2012). Reviving Papert's dream. *Educational Technology, 52*(4), 42–46. Retrieved from web.media.mit.edu/~mres/papers/educational-technology-2012.pdf

Rodríguez, D. (2009). Implications of culturally and linguistically diverse students with autism. *Early Childhood 85*(9), 313–317.

Rodríguez, D., Ringler, M., O'Neal, D., & Bunn, K. (2009). Academic factors indicating successful programs for English language learners. *Journal of Research in Childhood Education, 23*(4), 512–525.

Schweizer, T., Ware, J., Fischer, E., Fergus, I. M. C., & Bialystok, E. (2011). Bilingualism as a contributor to cognitive reserve: Evidence from brain atrophy in Alzheimer's disease. *Cortex, 48*(8), 991–996.

Seifoori, Z., Mozaheb, M. A., & Beigi, A. B. (2012). A profile of an effective EFL writing teacher: A technology-based approach. *English Language Teaching, 5*(5), 107–117.

Sessoms, D. (2008). Interactive instruction: Creating interactive learning environments through tomorrow's teachers. *International Journal of Technology in Teaching and Learning, 4*(2), 86–96.

Shapiro, M. (2004). How including prior knowledge as a subject variable may change outcomes of learning research. *American educational Research Journal, 41*(1), 159–189.

Sherris, A. (2008). *Integrated content and language instruction.* Retrieved from www.cal.org/resources/digest/integratedcontent.html

Short, D., Fidelman, C., & Louguit, M. (2012). Developing academic language in English language learners through sheltered instruction. *TESOL Quarterly, 46*(2), 334–361.

Shulman, L. (1981). *Techniques and applications of path integration.* New York: Wiley.

Skow, L., & Stephan, L. (2000). Intercultural communication in the university classroom. In L. A. Samovar & R. E. Porter (Eds.), *Intercultural communication* (9th ed., pp 355–370). Belmont, CA: Wadsworth.

Slavin, R., & Calderón, M. (Eds.) (2001). *Effective programs for Latino students.* Mahwah, NJ: Lawrence Erlbaum Associates.

Smiley, P., & Salsberry, T. (2007). *Effective schooling for English language learners: What elementary principals should know and do.* Larchmont, NY: Eye on Education.

Smith, P. H., & Arnot-Hopffer, E. (1998). Exito bilingue: Promoting Spanish literacy in a dual language immersion program. *Bilingual Research Journal, 22*, 103–119.

Snow, M. A. (2005). A model of academic literacy for integrated language and content instruction. In E. Hinkel (Ed.), *Handbook of research in second language learning* (pp. 693–712). Mahwah, NJ: Erlbaum.

Soltero, S. (2004). *Dual language teaching and learning in two languages.* New York: Pearson.

Soto, L. (1997). *Language, culture, and power: Bilingual families and the struggle for quality education.* Albany, NY: State University of New York.

Stewart, J. H. (2005). Foreign language study in elementary schools: Benefits and implications for achievement in reading and math. *Early Childhood Education Journal, 33*, 11–16.

Sugerman, J., & Howard, L. (2001). *Two-way immersion shows promising results: Findings from a new study.* Washington, DC: Center for Applied Linguistics.

The Civil Rights Act 1964, 42 U.S.C. § 2000d.

The Rehabilitation Act of 1973, Section 504 Regulations, 34 C.F.R. §1-4.1 *et seq.*

Thomas, W., & Collier, V. (1997). *School effectiveness for language minority students.* Washington, DC: National Clearinghouse for Bilingual Education.

Thomas, W., & Collier, V. (2000). Accelerated schooling for all students: Research findings on education in multilingual communities. In S. Shaw (Ed.), *Intercultural education in European classrooms.* Stoke-on-Trent, UK: Trentham Books.

Thomas, W., & Collier, V. (2002). *National study of school effectiveness for language minority students' long-term academic achievement: Final report.* Santa Cruz, CA: Center for Research on Education, Diversity and Excellence.

Thomas, W., & Collier, V. (2003a). The multiple benefits of dual language. *Educational Leadership, 61*(2), 61–64

Thomas, W., & Collier, V. (2003b). *A national study of school effectiveness for language minority students' long-term academic achievement.* Washington, DC: Center for Research on Education, Diversity & Excellence. Retrieved from www.crede.ucsc.edu/research/llaa/1.1_final.html

Thonis, E. (1986). Reading instruction for language minority students. In California State Department of Education Office of Bilingual Bicultural Education, *Schooling and language minority students: A theoretical framework* (pp. 147–181). Los Angeles, CA: Evaluation, Dissemination and Assessment Center, California State University.

Tompkins, G. (2001). *Literacy for the 21st century: A balanced approach.* Upper Saddle River, NJ: Prentice Hall.

Tunmer, W. E., & Myhill, M. E. (1984). Metalinguistic awareness and bilingualism. In W. E. Tunmer, C. Pratt, & M. L. Herriman (Eds.), *Metalinguistic awareness in children.* Berlin: Springer Verlag.

UNESCO. (1953). *The use of vernacular languages in education.* Retrieved from unesdoc.unesco.org/images/0000/000028/002897eb.pdf

UNESCO. (2003). Education in a multilingual world. Retrieved from unesdoc.unesco.org/images/0012/001297/129728e.pdf

U.S. Department of Education. (n.d.). *Learning: Engage and empower.* Retrieved from www.ed.gov/technology/netp-2010/learning-engage-and-empower

Vacca, R. T., & Vacca, J. L. (2004). *Content area reading: Literacy and learning across the curriculum* (8th ed.). Boston, MA: Allyn & Bacon.

Vacca, R.T., Vacca, J. L., & Begoray, D. L. (2005). *Content area reading: Literacy and learning across the curriculum.* Ontario, CN: Pearson Education Canada Inc.

Vaid, J., & Hull, R. (2001). *A tale of two hemispheres: A meta-analytic review of the bilingual brain of language-minority students.* Poster presented at the Third Symposium on Bilingualism, University of the West of England.

Valdés, G. (1997). The teaching of Spanish to bilingual Spanish-speaking students: Outstanding issues and unanswered questions. In M. C. Colombia & F. X. Alarcón (Eds.), *La enseñanza del español a hispanohablantes* (pp. 8–44). Boston, MA: Houghton Mifflin Company.

Valle, J. W., & Conner, D. J. (2011). *Rethinking disability.* New York: McGraw Hill.

Van den Akker, J. (1999). Principles and methods of development research. In J. van den Akker, N. Nieveen, R. M. Branch, K. L. Gustafson, & T. Plomp (Eds.), *Design methodology and developmental research in education and training* (pp. 1–14). Dordrecht, Netherlands: Kluwer Academic Publishers.

Viadero, D. (2009). *Research hones focus on ELLs.* Retrieved from www.edweek.org/ew/articles/2009/01/08/17research.h28.html

Villa, D. J. (2002). Integrating technology into minority language preservation and teaching efforts: An inside job. *Language Learning, & Technology* 6(2), 92–101.

Vygotsky, L. (1962). *Thought and language*. Cambridge, MA: MIT Press.

Vygotsky, L. (1978). *Mind in society*. Cambridge, MA: Harvard University Press.

Vygotsky, L. (2005). Interaction between learning and development. In P. Richard-Amato & M. Snow (Ed.), *Academic success for English language learners: Strategies for K–12 mainstream teachers* (pp. 103-111). White Plains, NY: Pearson Education.

Walker-Dalhouse, D. (2008). Where life and children's literature meet: Creating a potential bridge to understand the lives of elementary age African American males. In W. Brooks and J. McNair, *Embracing, evaluating, and examining the lives of African-American children's and young adult literature*. Lanham, MD: Scarecrow Press.

Wang, F., & Hannafin, M. J. (2005). Design-based research and technology-enhanced learning environments. *Educational Technology Research and Development, 53(4),* 5–23.

Wang, Q., Shao, Y., & Li, Y. J. (2010). "My mom or mom's way"? The bilingual and bicultural self in Hong Kong Chinese children and adolescents. *Child Development, 81*(2), 555–567.

Weaver, C. (1988). *Reading process and practice*. Portsmouth, NH: Heinemann.

Wong Fillmore, L. (2004). *The role of language in academic development*. Santa Rosa, CA: Sonoma County Office of Education.

Yum, J. (2000). The impact of Confucianism on interpersonal relationships and communication patterns in East Asia. In L. A. Samovar & R. E. Porter (Eds.), *Intercultural communication* (9th ed., pp. 63–73). Belmont, CA: Wadsworth.

Zentella, A. (1997). *Growing up bilingual: Puerto Rican children in New York*. Oxford: Blackwell Publishers.

Zhang, C., & Cho, S. (2010). The development of the bilingual special education field: Major issues, accomplishments, future, directions, and recommendations. *Journal of Multilingual Education Research, 1,* 45–62.

Index

About the Authors

Diane Rodríguez is an associate professor at Fordham University, Graduate School of Education. She specializes in the areas of bilingual special education, bilingual education, and second language teaching and learning. Dr. Rodríguez has been invited to speak at national and international conferences on special education and bilingual education. Dr. Rodríguez's publications include the articles "Meeting the Needs of English Language Learners with Disabilities in Urban Settings" (*Urban Education Journal*); "English Language Learners with Disabilities' Interpretation of Word Problem Solving in Middle Schools" (*The Bolder Walking Journal*); "Implications of Culturally and Linguistically Diverse Students with Autism" (*Early Childhood*); and "Academic Factors Indicating Successful Programs for English Language Learners" (*Journal of Research in Childhood Education*).

Angela Carrasquillo, the Claudio Aquaviva Distinguished Professor of TESOL at Fordham University Graduate School of Education, retired 3 years ago but continues her involvement as an educational consultant and program evaluator. She is nationally known in the area of second language and bilingual education and has published extensively on these topics. Dr. Carrasquillo's publications include *Between Puerto Rico and New York: A Latina Professor's Journey* (2011); *Beyond the Beginnings: Literacy Interventions for Upper Elementary English Language Learners* (with Stephen Kucer & Ruth Abrams, 2004); and *Language Minority Students in the Mainstream Classroom* (with Vivian Rodriguez, 2002).

Kyung Soon Lee is an adjunct professor at Touro College, School of Education. Dr. Lee specializes in the teaching of bilingual and TESOL courses, especially in methods for teaching native language arts and the teaching of English language learners in the content areas. Dr. Lee presents at local and state organizations in the areas of cultural and linguistic characteristics of Korean students and methodological approaches in teaching bilingual and English language learners. Her publications include "Korean College Students in the United States: Perceptions of Professors and Students" (*College Student Journal*) and "Korean College Students Learning Mode and English Communication: Voices of Korean College Students in the United States" (*Korean Society of Quality Relationships [KSQR]*).

DATE DUE

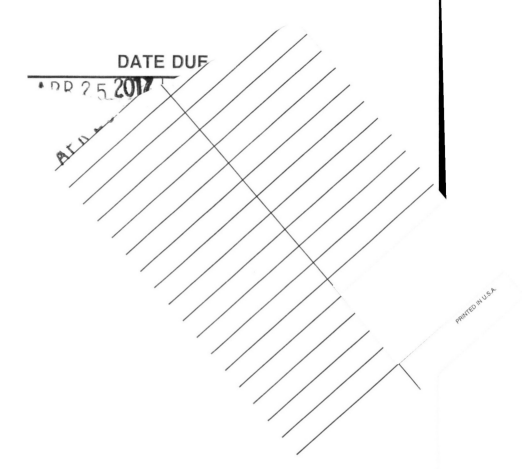

APR 25 2017

PRINTED IN U.S.A.